Stairway from Heaven

By Linda Kobler

Published by Eternal, an Imprint of
DragonEye Publishing

Stairway from Heaven, by Linda Kobler
Copyright © 2016, by Linda Kobler.

Published by
Eternal, an Imprint of DragonEye Publishing

First Edition:
First Printing October 1, 2016

ISBN 13: 978-1-61500-130-9 (Paperback)
ISBN 13: 978-1-61500-132-3 (EBook Mobi)
ISBN 13: 978-1-61500-136-1 (Ebook EPub)

Library of Congress Control Number: 2016952845

Publisher info. Contact
DragonEye Publishing
511 W. Water St., Unit E
Elmira, New York, 14905

Phone: 1-(607)-333-5256
Website: DragonEyePublishers.com
Orders@DragonEyePublishers.com

Table of Contents

DEDICATION

For my wonderful parents and their adoring, endless love.

For my sister Judy who shared my childhood so lovingly.

For my husband David who makes all my dreams come true.

For my darlings, Jeremie, Matthew and Jason, my precious sons who have given me the greatest joy in my life.

For my beautiful seven grandchildren who keep me forever young and fill my life with magic.

"*For where your treasure is, there will your heart be also.*"
MATTHEW 6:21

In loving remembrance of SGT. Jeremie James Kobler

11-10-73 to 9-26-12

ACKNOWLEDGEMENTS

I AM FOREVER grateful to the many contributors who shared their miraculous encounters and testimonies with me, allowing the world a luminous glimpse beyond death.

Judy Lamz Tilton, Sam Brinez, Ruth Roy, Karen Swinford, Judi and Harvey Meadvin, Mary Brickley, Rodney Baker, Rosalie Balcitis, Arturo Elpidio, Patricia Dace, Pat, Elizenda V. Marquez Clover, Barb Martinez, Alice Stacionis, Deborah Meeks and William Kocureck. Some names were withheld by request.

Special appreciation to all my wonderful friends, sons Jason and Matthew, sister Judy and coworkers who generously allowed me to consult with them endlessly on the writing and the review of *STAIRWAY from HEAVEN*.

Loving thanks to my amazing husband David with whose assistance in formatting, editing, cover design and all endeavors made this book possible.

PREFACE

I BELIEVE THAT we are timeless, the great mystery which has perplexed mankind since the beginning of human existence. Immortality and the proof of it has mystified and intrigued all cultures and civilizations since the beginning of time.

In 2016, more than half of us believe that spiritual forces have influence on the earth. Research commissioned to launch a podcast *THINGS UNSEEN,* revealed that 16% of those surveyed reported that they knew someone who had experienced a miracle. 8% of the nonreligious reported that they or someone they knew had experienced a miracle.

Research regarding religion around the world reveals that 63% of the population is religious, 22% is nonreligious and 11% is atheist. (The Independent, April 2015).

According to Theos (Religious Think Tank) a majority of people (59%) are believers in the existence of some kind of spiritual beings.

Although institutionalized religious belonging has declined over recent decades, the world has not become nonreligious. On the contrary, a spiritual current runs powerfully throughout an enlightening world.

The research also reveals that more than three in five Christians (62%) believe that spiritual forces influence people's thoughts and the human or natural world.

More surprisingly, 35% of the nonreligious believe this as well.

We find reference to the human spirit throughout both the Old and New Testament.

According to the bible, *"the dust of the ground"* *becomes the physical body and a "living soul"* refers to the human soul, which is one's psychological part, their mind, emotion and will. The breath of life refers to the third part of man, that of the human spirit. Proverbs 20:27 says *"The spirit of man is the lamp of Jehovah."*

A survey in 2012 revealed that 55% of those polled believe in life after death, 58% believe in Heaven and 72% believe in the human soul. 63% report a belief in communication between the living and the departed.

Of the latter, 51% report a personal experience and communication with a deceased loved one.

Each one of us must decide for ourselves what the human spirit actually is. Is it the part of us that continues after death? The presenters in this book will accompany you on a mesmerizing journey. Their true story accounts will offer you a new look at spiritual events and visitation after death.

Once published, my first book, SACRED MESSAGES took on a life of its own. A flood of personal testimonies and magnificent validations emerged.

I came to realize the overwhelming interest in the quest for spiritual knowledge. Nearly half of all humans will have a spiritual experience in their lifetime. Many events will be shared from generation to generation. Some will be quietly whispered within family walls. Others will be declared in legend or find a place in history. Often the testimonies will be poignant, rare or perhaps miraculous in nature. These accounts open doors to a sacred place, one many of us wonder of, long for and seek.

Science is beginning to acknowledge the possibility of spiritual and mystical events, facts that the ancients have known time immemorial.

It seems only to follow that one day science and spiritualism will join in agreement that these resplendent events are not only *real,* but actually quite common and experienced frequently by those who have the ability to *perceive them.*

One must open their eyes to see, miracles happen every day.

STAIRWAY FROM HEAVEN is a spellbinding collection, an anthology of miraculous true stories of spiritual encounters.

The individuals who presented their moving experiences wished to offer hope, validation and the promise of life after life.

Following the death of our eldest son, Jeremie, our eyes were opened, never to close again.

I continue to share his resplendent message of hope and life after life. As a beacon of light, Jeremie's love continues to burn ever so brightly.

As the door opens and the pages turn, we invite you to a transforming odyssey. Our hope is that the skeptic will be enlightened, the grieving will find hope and our loved ones, no longer with us will find their way home.

Stairway
from
Heaven

11 - 12 - 16

A mi maravillosa Amigo
Sam - con gratitud y Amor,

"It was a small copper coin floating magically through the air, resting finally on my pillow. I knew it to be a gift from my brother, his promise that we are never parted."

The Brothers

"WHERE THERE IS SHADOW,
LIGHT."

FROM THE PRAYER OF ST. FRANCIS

THE KISS

"LIFE IS SPIRIT. IT FLOWS THROUGH THE
DEATH OF ME, ENDLESSLY, LIKE A RIVER
UNAFRAID OF BECOMING THE SEA."

Costa

Chapter 1

THE HEAVY DOORS bursting open, she entered as if launched by a massive wind. Somewhat frenzied and disordered, she anxiously searched the store, hoping to find her point of mission. As she turned the corner, our eyes met and the young woman seemed to float toward me. Suddenly she appeared directly facing me, her hand firmly placed on my book. She trembled with excitement and her voice though audible, delivered her message in whispered tones. "He is here you know, the man in the book. Is he your son?" I responded that yes, my son was presented in the book. By this time, the other authors and the crowd began to draw closer, in the hope of hearing her excited, yet subdued declaration. I explained to the woman that my son, Jeremie, had died tragically two years before and was the inspiration for the book, *Sacred Messages*. She nodded in agreement and pointed into the store "He is here with me today and he wants me to deliver a message to you."

There had been an electric charge in the air that morning. This was the initial book signing for *Sacred Messages*, my first book.

Barnes and Noble had invited several local authors in the Rockford, Illinois area. I was very excited to be included. I hurried about, unpacking my case, seeking my assigned seating area, placing my book marks, business cards and display items on the presentation table. Pen readied, I eagerly anticipated the first signing of my book.

Once settled, I began chatting with two of the authors. Having attended other book signings, they were more experienced at these events. I welcomed their advice and direction and we made plans for lunch at a future date. We conversed, presented our books and wandered throughout the store, marketing our written wares to literary lovers. A few readers shopped for a gift, a daunting endeavor as most individuals are often quite particular regarding their personal reading preferences. Some were students, others adventure seekers.

Of course there was always the quiet pensive who sought the perfect book to read by the fire while sipping a glass of wine.

Which of them would be the reader for my book?

I had never imagined writing a book or ever really being an author. Having always loved writing, I had enjoyed some elemental attempts at poetry in my teenage years.

I had written and presented eulogies for both of my wonderful parents and my Aunt Rose.

I have authored all of our family's annual Christmas letters for the past forty years, some out of a sense of holiday obligation yet, mostly for my own personal enjoyment.

I was the dedicated amateur, to be sure, and have enjoyed writing letters to friends and family, despite the tempting convenience of computers and Facebook. Old fashioned, I suppose, the art of letter writing and the beauty of the written word has always been my preference. The mastery of the script and the flow of each word bequeaths a more personal, memorable and lasting presence not found in contemporary communication.

One rainy afternoon, three years ago, I discovered an old dusty wooden box in our attic, one that my mother must have saved from my youth. It was an amazing find as I had never seen it before.

Inside were crayoned notes to my parents and sister Judy, little scribbled sketches of the sun, clouds, figure drawings and primary diaries from the first grade when I was five. The written word has become a way of life for me, I suppose, jotting notes on the back of check books, napkins or any little scrap of paper available. I have even resorted to noting on the bottoms of my shoes when necessary.

If a special quote, thought or song dances through my head it becomes noteworthy and is promptly added to the archives for later scrutiny.

I had also written journals throughout the years when my children were small, starting months before they were born and into their childhoods. My journals are now waning and weathered, yet never fail to resurrect tender memories each time they are read. So perhaps in some universal way, the potential for writing lies in all of us.

We collect thoughts and memorabilia in tiny boxes under our beds or in forgotten closets with the intention of revisiting them one day and entreating them to permanence. As the mute who chooses not to speak, sings only when the music demands lyrics.

Journaling is an ancient art. There exists evidence of writing dating back to Mesopotamia (Sumer) in 3200 BCE and Meso-America in 600 BC. An ancient diary and collection of letters written by Pliny the Youngers in 79 AD described the disaster in Pompeii and was not discovered until the sixteenth century. The Bible itself is a collection of sixty six books written by forty authors over a sixteen hundred year period. The written word can cease time, heal wounds of the soul or register history. It allows one the opportunity to transfer emotion to writing and reflect it from one's heart.

Writing eternalizes the human experience, in love, war, religion, personal joy and tragedy. Journaling became my obsession in an effort to express and reconcile my anguish.

David and I were blessed with three sons. It has been said that each child bequeaths its mother a spiritual lesson. The new born is the most relentless of teachers.

A young mother so wanting to prove herself worthy and competent, dedicates her very existence to her precious new charge. In the intensity of this sacred relationship, I believe that the infant and the mother merge into one spiritual entity.

The sanctity and miracle of gestation and birth creates a constancy in this amazing union, although different souls, one divine inseparable connection and one shared spirit from conception to eternity. It is a bond like no other in human existence. The love between mother and child is endless and transcends death. The young soldier calls out to his mother in the last throws of death as the mother's last words are those of love for her children.

The greatest of all love stories is that between a mother and child.

And so it would be with my three sons, sacred tributaries blooming from the main tree, their mother, intertwined eternally in her branches and though separate, intermingled to their origin.

With the blessing of the sun's light and its kiss of warmth, three young, stronger and beautiful trees emerge to grow and flourish. Hence, our children became my *Corazon, mon tout, my everything,*

From the moment our sons were born, they became David's and my morning, our good night and everything in between. My total happiness and joy of life has always revolved around the family, once our beautiful babies and in the passing of time, our amazing grown men, our trio of sons, and the Kobler band of brothers.

They have been the music to my song. Jeremie, Matthew and Jason became David's and my life's purpose. Motherhood has been my reason for being.

My name was announced over the store's PA system and it was time for my presentation at last. I began to describe the book. It is a unique book in that it is a love story, a memoir and a mystery. It describes my early years and the amazing spiritual history of my family. My mother, and both of my grandmothers were spiritually gifted. The story is true and describes mystical and miraculous events in my life that are unexplained.

Following the tragic death of our son, Jeremie, amazing events began to occur.

We received numerous letters, emails and phone calls from his friends, co-workers family and acquaintances, describing dreams and communications which were spellbinding.

It was incredible and these amazing messages inspired "*SACRED MESSAGES.*"

The audience seemed intrigued and began purchasing books and specifying their requests for my signature.

Many readers shared their personal stories with me, describing their own tragic losses. They were people searching for comfort, for answers. They hoped for miracles, just as I had after the death of our son, Jeremie. I signed their books and I wished them peace and the hope that the book would give them a new way of looking at loss. I encouraged them to be vigilant, to be aware of messages, though perhaps unexplained, *actual* spiritual communications. Miracles happen every day, one must open their eyes to see, one must trust in that which is unseen and unexplained.

I had recalled all the years of my childhood, being aware of miraculous events and witnessing many of them for myself. One by one, the words of my mother, her reassuring smile and mystical predictions became an intrinsic part of me. My own precognitive dreams pronounced my belief.

I knew deep in my heart that wondrous events happen every day, that skeptics will always shake their heads and one should not be discouraged by them.

There *are* unexplained mysteries in this earthly existence which are not understood or easily explained, yet actually *do* occur.

I believe our eyes are finally opened to Sacred Messages following a tragic loss, a life changing illness or the observation of an amazing event that cannot be easily explained. My religious education and my experiences as an adult have convinced me;

"We are not humans having a spiritual existence, but spiritual beings having a human existence."(Pierre De Chardin)

The tragic, sudden death of our son, Jeremie, forever changed me. A trip to the local apple orchard on a warm September afternoon would end in tragedy. Having survived three deployments to the Middle East, seventeen years in the Air Force and nineteen tears in law enforcement it all seemed too impossible to believe.

One moment he was happily riding his motorcycle on a country road, the next, so badly broken and wounded that he died instantly. My grief and sense of loss was paralyzing. I clung to my faith blindly, in complete surrender. There were to be no final goodbyes, no last words of love, no adoring embrace. Our wonderful Jeremie was gone.

The tears flowed from my pen, bleeding onto the paper, transforming as ink. I was consumed in capturing these experiences, to put the pain to paper, to establish a record and a mirror to our crippling loss.

The early months of journaling after Jeremie's death were fogged and blurred, as I struggled with my grief.

My anguish created the words and my sorrow, the paragraphs. In a brief few months, my expose' was complete, my heart unveiled and transparent, hence my torture had come to light for all the world to witness.

SACRED MESSAGES emerged as the book that wrote me.

While in the Air Force on various deployments, Jeremie had always found a way to communicate with his father and I, to tell us he was safe. One email cited "**JKOK**". This was offered at a time of military action. Another message sent was "**SOON**". "**SWAK**" and "**KISS**".

I knew in my mother's heart that my son would find a way to come home to me, a way to comfort us, to reassure us that he was "OK". His resplendent image in the evergreen tree overlooking the funeral service affirmed what I had prayed for. Jeremie had transcended death to offer this one last gift, this message of love, this proof of immortality.

Friends, family, and coworkers called, wrote and emailed endlessly with dreams of Jeremie communicating after his death. Amazingly, the communications continue regularly after several years.

Jeremie's death was my darkest hour. The greatest torture was the recurring thought of my wonderful son dying on the cold, filthy road, alone and suffering unimaginable, grueling pain the long minutes before he died. There had been no one to comfort him, to hold him in a last embrace, to speak the words of love and prayer. The thought haunted me, vexing my sleep and my peace and remained ever present in my mind.

The impression of Jeremie dying alone in hideous pain had been a perpetual sword in my heart.

The young dark haired woman continued to whisper her golden words, mesmerizing me, our eyes locked in hypnotic focus. For several endless minutes, I was oblivious to anything or anyone around me. There was only this hushed miracle, this mystical bestowal filling my heart and exhilarating my very soul. Impervious, I studied every breath she took, the resonance of her voice and every word she spoke. I was compelled to enshrine it to memory as if in the listening, my Jeremie would return to me.

Her name was Mercedes and she shared the fact that she had been a visionary, a psychic medium since the age of twelve. She remembered being quite ill as a child and felt perhaps that was the beginning of her "gift." She continued," some people call me a diviner or conjurer.

Most of my communication with spirit is dark and full of despair, very sad. However this message was the most beautiful I have ever received, so full of love and light that I had to make this journey to deliver it to you." As she spoke the tears danced down her face and the two of us wept together.

She continued. "Last evening, my family and I were having dinner in a restaurant in Aurora Illinois. It was exactly 5:30PM on September 26th, 2014. I believe that it was the second anniversary of your son's death and the exact time of his death, yes?" (I nodded in agreement, incredulous at her knowing these details as she had not read the book.) "At that very moment a tall, dark haired man walked past our table, dressed in a military uniform. He was really extraordinary, young and handsome wearing medals and an Air Force beret.

The insignia on his uniform was "Air Force Security Police"; the name badge was KOBLER. As he passed us I believed him to be of flesh as he was solid, as if not spiritual. Then he turned to smile at me and he was encircled by a beautiful white light and I knew him to be spirit.

He spoke no words but delivered this message; "Tell my family and children that I love them and I am happy and well, I am waiting for them here." He made a motion from his lips   and blew it as if a Kiss. He smiled and continued with the message. "Just for my mother, please tell her that I did not suffer or feel any pain at the accident. I had already been liberated from my body before the impact.

I witnessed the accident from above and there was no pain. Please tell my mother that I love her and not to mourn. Tell her I am happy." With that the young airman smiled, turned, thanked her and vanished.

I sat stunned, spellbound with her testimony. This message could only have come from my Jeremie. Only *he* would have known my deepest wound, my persistent nightmare, my haunting worry.

I asked the medium how it was that she knew her destination and how to find me? She answered "Spirit always guides me. I got into my car this morning and began driving toward Rockford. I was guided to the bookstore by the young airman and as I approached the book store, saw him waiting for me at the doors". She explained that she had not read the book and knew nothing of it.

Her only mission was to deliver this precious message from a son to his mother, this loving, amazing message of hope and light. "It is a gift of love to you, because he loves you so much."

These events were the revelation and inspiration for the sequel, STAIRWAY from HEAVEN.

"He said softly, "I love you Mother." He took my hand and kissed it, then folded my fingers around the stem of the rose. He had stripped it of its thorns."

Elizabeth Peters

MY PRAYER

"I BELIEVE IN PRAYER.

IT IS THE BEST WAY TO

DRAW STRENGTH FROM

HEAVEN."

Josephine Baker

Chapter 2

ROSALIE BALCITIS ADORED her wonderful parents. Growing up, she loved the traditional celebrations and the joy of everyday life with her family.

Time passed and Rosalie left her childhood home and married. Two years later, her father died when her son was nine months old. The loss tormented the family. Now, Shirley, Rosalie's mother, would remain the matriarch, her only living parent. Needless to say, Shirley became the primary focus and treasure of the family.

In 1999, on a warm summer afternoon, Rosalie's mother suffered a tragic accident. While crossing the road, Shirley was struck by a car.

It was a miracle that she had survived. Injured, it seemed, beyond recovery, Rosalie's mother clung precipitously to life. Broken and comatose, death beckoned.

"I spent every hour with my mother, day and night, never leaving her side. After two days at her bed side, I risked a visit to the hospital chapel. I was exhausted and consumed with worry and fear. I began to pray."

Deep in prayer for several minutes, Rosalie became aware of a presence in the chapel. So dedicated to her mission, she continued with her prayer and dedication, believing that the presence was someone else's suffering family member seeking comfort.

Softly, Rosalie felt a touch to her shoulder. A soft voice whispered compassionately, as if calming a weeping child.

The words were very clear and precise, *"your mother will live."*

Rosalie knew it to be the presence of an angel. She felt the hands on her shoulders and the softness of breath upon her face.

Rosalie opened her eyes, searching the empty chapel and running out into the hallways, only to discover no one there. She knew that the visit had been divine, giving hope to her grieving, anguished heart.

"Initially, I believed it to be a dream, and yet I knew that it was not. I knew it to be an actual physical experience and an amazing message to comfort me and render hope."

Miraculously, Rosalie's mother did in fact, survive. Physicians and hospital staff were amazed. After spending five months in the hospital for rehabilitation, Shirley Phillips returned home.

The sacred visitor in the hospital chapel had proclaimed and announced the incredible healing of Rosalie's mother.

"I have never again experienced anything like it. I know that the encounter in the chapel was heaven sent."

CALL HOME

"IT IS WITH OUR VOICES WE REMEMBER,

WITH OUR EARS WE UNDERSTAND."

Elizabeth Hunter

Chapter 3

THE 1970's SAW an explosion of amazing music, liberation in thinking and a freedom from social restraint never known before in society. It was the realization of a new age.

It was during these years that Lemar and Deborah met and fell in love. Lemar had been the high school jock. Unmatched in football, basketball and baseball, every sport he participated in became golden. Not only did he display excellence in sports, he was very bright and distinguished himself as an excellent student. Accomplished on the chess team as well, Lemar was a fine person and an impressive young man. Any young woman would have been delighted to spend time with him.

A few years later, Deborah and Lemar Meeks married. Happy and devoted to one another, they added two little ones to their family. Dreams coming true, life was wonderful.

Lemar continued to have a large circle of friends. Having a magnetic personality, he remained involved with old school buddies and would frequently meet the guys on week-ends for a basketball game, pool or a cold beer at the local pub and grill.

The gathering of old friends was important to Lemar. They would reminisce over the good old days. Revisiting his youth was a favorite pastime.

The relationships invited permanent youth and a true sense of camaraderie.

One Saturday afternoon such as this, the guys gathered at the pub. Lemar as usual, was the center of conversation, gregarious and entertaining.

Suddenly, without provocation, one of the old friends began to argue with the group. No one recalled the cause of the man's wrath, perhaps a misunderstanding?

The scenario quickly became violent when without explanation, the man drew a gun and shot Lemar. The well-loved and legendary young Lemar died at the scene.

The family in their anguish prepared for the funeral. Heart broken, Deborah and the children struggled to understand the tragic loss.

On the third day after Lemar's death, the family was spending time at an aunt's home. Loved ones offer a sanctuary to one another that is irreplaceable. No need for words, the silence and unspoken support is comforting enough.

The family painfully sorted through personal items and clothing while lost in thought and memories. The phone rang disturbing the calming silence.

Deborah answered the phone. It was Lemar's voice. He softly whispered "GOODBYE."

FLY AWAY

"BRING YOUR LOVE TO ME, AND I WILL
REMEMBER.

THEN I KNOW YOU MUST FLY AWAY."

Linda Kobler

Chapter 4

MY FATHER BELIEVED in the spiritual essence of birds. As we grew Daddy often shared stories with my sister and I, stories of birds carrying messages from loved ones no longer with us. These amazing birds were also capable of warnings and alerts of pending disaster and danger. These legendary communications were honored and well revered as they were believed to be heaven sent.

Several years after my father died I made the monthly journey to Daddy's and my mother's gravesite. Typically, planting flowers and removing old debris is the loving task of caring for a loved one's burial site. I believe that our loved ones spiritually move on from their place of rest, yet paying reverence to the grave is comforting to those of us who are left behind.

It had been a lovely fall day, painted with the crimson and golden colors of autumn. I traveled the one hour journey to the countryside to tend to my parent's gravesite.

The cemetery is located on a quiet country road, positioned on a slight elevation which is surrounded by wheat and corn fields.

The country side resembles a lovely painting, with its rolling hills, winding roads and ancient, massive oak trees.

The memorial park is archaic, serving as a sanctum to veterans of many wars; The Civil War, WW1 WW2, Korea and Viet Nam,   Sadly, there are more contemporary monuments as well, memorializing those veterans killed in wars of the Middle East.   My father was a well decorated veteran and hero of WW2. Consequently, Daddy and Mother loved this special place. My Uncle Wayne and my grandparents are also interred there.   One day, it will also be the final resting point for my husband, David and I. It is a mesmerizing, enchanted site.

Overlooking the cemetery on a cliffed   hill is an old country chapel. It has a quiet, haunting presence. Weathered and stressed, it serves as guardian to the hallowed grounds below it. It might easily have been the inspiration of poets.

I continued my task of grooming the ground and arranging the flowers. Without exception, tears always find my face when I visit my parent's graves.

Despite all the many years that have passed since their partings, the child in me still calls out with a longing for them.

Their love was all adoring and encompassing and inherently became a part of me.

My parents, Johnny and Dorothy Marquez achieved the highest rank of memorable, dedicated parents in the book of life.

Lost in thought and pensive, I was startled when a magnificent pheasant suddenly flew over my head, gently touching my hair with its beautiful wings. It turned and flew back over my head once more, this time gently touching my left shoulder. It then landed only a few feet from me. I was stunned.

We studied one another for several long seconds. The amazing bird was bejeweled in vibrant color. My heart still pounding, I stood frozen, afraid to move for fear of startling the bird and causing it to fly away.

As quietly as it had appeared, the spirit bird, as my father would call it, turned and vanished into the field.

Recalling the experience, I have never doubted the intention of that amazing encounter. The resplendent bird had been summoned by my father to deliver his message of love.

I have seen the bird only once, since, several years later. On October 12, as we drove to our granddaughter's, Madysen's fifth birthday party, a magnificent pheasant sat in the middle of the country road, requiring us to stop the car.

Once more, for several amazing seconds the bird studied us, then eventually flew off into the field.

As before, I believe the luminous bird had been sent by my father with a loving intention on a very special day.

Our granddaughter Madysen was born on October 12, a birthday she shares with my father, her great grandfather. The pheasant was my father's favorite bird, considering it to be the most spiritual of birds. Daddy's message of love was dedicated and tenderly delivered on his and his great granddaughter's birthday.

THE AWAKENING

"HE performs wonders that cannot be fathomed,
miracles that cannot be counted."

JOB 5:19

Chapter 5

CARLTON AND CHRISTINE BAKER enjoyed a large, loving family. Having realized the births of seven of their eleven children, family was their center and the primary focus of their lives.

Their home was electric with the sounds of children, the everyday hustle and bustle of a large family, the wonderful chaos, the music of children's voices and their enthusiasm for life. Growing up in a large household renders its own magic. One must learn to cooperate and conspire with one another in a significant way. It is an interdependence and symbiosis perhaps not experienced in smaller families. Sticking together is an absolute necessity.

Religion and a strong faith in the bible was also the core of the Baker family. Rodney reminisces about his grandmother, Cleota Guthrie, born in 1897 in Galva Illinois. "She was an amazing person, deeply religious and widely known for her prayers and healing ability. She was also psychic."

Cleota bequeathed her children and grandchildren with an unshakable belief in GOD. Sundays without fail, were reserved for church.

The Baker family assembled each Sunday at their regular church seating and worshipped. Cleota was very much at home in the old two story brick church. She drew her strength and her vision from the many hours of prayer in that holy place.

The weekly family worship was memorable. The Bakers would assemble to their regular seating, reputed to be thirty people, give or take, which often usurped one third of the church seating available. They were a force to be admired, this loving and dedicated family who attended each Sunday without exception.

Church was traditionally followed with a wonderful Sunday feast at Grandmother Cleota's house. It was tradition, the glue that binds, the gift of belonging. Cousins, aunts and uncles, siblings and grandparents were the circle of family.

They worshipped, celebrated and supported one another. Family was a sacred entity.

One chilly February afternoon in 1962, the Bakers traveled to Decatur Illinois to attend a special church revival. Christine Baker played the piano and organ beautifully and had been requested by her brother in law, Pastor Walter in Decatur, to play the organ at the large event. As her mother, Christine was devout in her faith and served as a wonderful role model to her children. Participating in the large revival would be her privilege.

They were excited and eager to visit with relatives not seen for some time. Having planned the short vacation for many months, they were well packed and the car was filled with snacks, hymnals and the Baker children.

Carlton would enjoy the time away from home, spending precious hours with his Christine and having the family all to himself for two days. The children, Rodney, Debbie and Larry rode in a separate car behind their parents with Uncle Fuzzy driving. The other children rode with their parents. Filled with anticipation and excitement, the caravan began their voyage.

The journey from Kiwanis to Decatur would take two hours. In the 1960's there were no super highways or interstates as we enjoy today. Stopping and starting through small towns with a myriad of truck stops and side roads would have been a challenge for drivers. Winter roads added to the difficulty.

Only one hour into their journey a sudden violent thrust propelled the vehicle into a culvert. Crashing into the ditch, Carlton Baker was thrown from the car. The tire had exploded, causing the accident.

Christine had been trapped in the twisted wreckage, tossed about the vehicle as if a butterfly in a storm. Kevin, age 5, had minor injuries. The children were able to exit the car and were amazingly unharmed. The ambulance screaming, the lifesaving procedures began for Carlton. Unconscious and bleeding heavily, his pelvis fractured, he was rushed off to the hospital.

Hopelessly injured and broken, Christine was declared dead at the accident site.

The tragic news was staggering. The remainder of the Baker family was notified immediately after the collision. They would be able to reach the hospital quickly and care for the children who were horribly traumatized. On this horrible day, life had forever changed for the wonderful Baker family.

Cleota rushed to Hopedale Hospital. Heart pounding, terror realized, she began fervently to pray. Bolting into the hospital, she found her precious daughter lying dead in the hallway.

Christine was cold and lifeless, lying on a cart and covered with a sheet. Cleota, two of her brothers and sisters and Pastor Walter removed the cover and laid across Christine's body. They prayed intensely for forty five minutes. They prayed on their knees, while embracing their loved one, calling desperately but assuredly to GOD to restore sacred breath to this wonderful young mother and daughter.

Then came the miracle of miracles. Christine stirred. Sacred breath returned, GOD had answered their prayers. The young woman was once more, alive.

Christine's miraculous awakening was proclaimed by the medical staff as a true miracle. Amazed, the physicians agreed that it had been the prayers and the love and dedication of her family that had returned her to life.

Christine recovered for four long arduous months in the hospital. Having suffered severe injuries, her healing was long and painful. This second chance at life and the births of four children in the years to follow was validation enough that Christine was exactly where she was intended to be. The miraculous awakening was her destiny.

Christine Baker is now in her eighties. She remains devout in her faith as was her mother before her. She enjoys her children and grandchildren. She never misses church. Always with her is the remembrance of her awakening. Precious life continued, prayer remains the center of her life.

"AND NOW WE STEP TO THE RHYTHM OF MIRACLES

FROM THE LIGHT THAT NEVER DIES."

Aberjham

Sacred Coins

"WHAT WE HAVE ONCE ENJOYED WE CAN
NEVER LOSE;

ALL THAT WE LOVE BECOMES A PART OF US."

Helen Keller

Chapter 6

MARIO AND SARAH had fallen in love. It happened one magical summer night when moonlight discovers young dreamers wishing on a star. They were very young and love was so new. Their freshman year soon to begin, they were destined to begin this milestone, hand in hand, the two of them against the world.

It had been so tender, so exciting, first a glance, then a smile and ultimately the connection that draws us to one another out of the thousands of encounters we each experience. The two teenagers had experienced that undeniable spiritual magnetism to one another.

Mario and Sarah would be high school sweethearts. It was true love, their first serious experience in romance. Dramatic and tender, first love always renders a memorable experience. It had been love at first sight. Little notes in her locker, stolen kisses in the halls and the promise of a movie on Saturday night.

Their adoring glances to one another would resonate into winter afternoons and enchant the warm summer nights. New love was exhilarating to the young lovers.

They quoted poetry on the phone, sang love songs to one another and dreaming of their futures, shared their hopes and plans. There was the promise of life together, the vision of marriage and children. They were sheltered in the enchantment of one another. Life was endless and ever so sweet.

They had each other as a sanctuary and the world was a wondrous, protected, amazing place.

As the two graduated from high school and left for college, a separation ensued, yet with the pledge of spending summers and vacations together. Parting was painful and rendered a longing for one another. Letters and phone calls continued the romance, despite the distance and separation. Sacred memories were collected in shoe boxes and drawers.

Gradually, over the months, the phone calls and letters dwindled, eventually ceasing. Life demands began to overshadow the young romance.

Life and education and the myriad of responsibilities overshadowed the tender love story.

As the years passed hurriedly by Mario and Sarah went off in different directions. The memory of their first romance however, had become an intrinsic part of their beings. They had dedicated several precious years of their lives to one another during a magical time.

There would remain a bond between them that time and other loves would not erase.

Time passed.

A few years later Sarah received a phone call. It was the call we all fear. It is the pronouncement that is life changing. Mario had been struck and tragically killed in a car accident.

Time stood still. Remembrances flooded Sarah's mind. Tears flowed. How does one close the door to one's youth and first love? Mario had shared his dream of becoming an artist and opening his own studio. These plans were never to be. The wonderful young man whom Sarah had loved was now gone, his life, ended.

Sarah suffered, knowing that Mario's death would leave a painful void in her life.

Sadly, this wonderful person would remain only a loving memory. The sorrow was overwhelming.

After the funeral and the days following, Sarah realized the finality of her loss. Those we love become a part of us. The passing stranger who offers a smile is not incidental. Every encounter and friendship spiritually binds us to one another in a significant way. She realized that Mario's absence would leave a void in her life. We are all connected, despite the endings and the beginnings.

Sarah began to pray, hoping that Mario was safe and well.

The concern and grief haunted her, every day at work, while on the train and as she lay quietly in her bed at night. She began the sacred conversations, the ones we utter under our breath, whispers that are meant for spiritual ears only "please hear me, Mario and know that I have always loved you, Please give me a sign that you are happy and safe."

Sarah remembers "I suddenly began finding random dimes, so frequently that I began to seriously take notice. I researched the possibility that the coins were in fact a spiritual communication.

I discovered that passed loved ones often send coins as a form of comfort to those of us left behind. The little coins were a bridge between us, one world to the other. Mario sent this message to me to prove that he is well. This was an amazing gift to confirm my belief in the beyond. I continue to receive the dimes during key times in my life. We remain together, one world to the other, though apart."

GIFTS FROM BEYOND

'WE ARE IGNORANT OF THE BEYOND
BECAUSE THIS IGNORANCE IS THE
CONDITION OF OUR LIFE,
JUST AS ICE CANNOT KNOW FIRE
EXCEPT BY VANISHING."
Julian Renard

Chapter 7

WHEN JUDI MAAS MEADVIN was six years old, her father died suddenly. This tragedy and loss at such a tender age left her confused and overwhelmed with the longing for her father. Understanding death for a young child is perplexing and incomprehensible. The concept of death is difficult and unexplainable to small children. Loss yields a mighty blow to such a little person.

Judi recalls the painful memories following her father's death, "Needless to say, I did not have a clear understanding of what had happened and why my Daddy was no longer here. People remarked that he was sleeping or that he had gone to Heaven to live with Jesus. Why wouldn't he wake up? I needed him here, holding and loving me, living in our house where we had all been so happy. I needed my father more than Jesus did! Mother stopped speaking of his death, perhaps in an attempt to cause my brother and I less pain. Unfortunately, her decision to block my father's death only caused more anguish for us."

Edwin Maas was a WW2 veteran, having served as an engine mechanic while in Germany. He was a patriot and loved his country. Dedicated and hardworking, he was happy to care for and provide for his family. Life was simple for Edwin.

He enjoyed hunting and spending time on his family farm. Collectively, the Maas family owned a vast complex of acreage in the Portage Wisconsin area. Judi remembers long walks in the woods with her father, picking apples and picnics in the summer. "Daddy would say to be quiet and hear the woods talking. He taught me a love and appreciation of nature that has remained a gift throughout my life."

Judi describes the sweet demeanor of her father. "My favorite memory was one special night when Daddy called my nick name, Toupie, wake up…and I became aware of a warm, sweet smelling puppy licking my nose. We named him Lucky because Daddy said we were both lucky to have each other, the puppy and I. It was a wonderful gift from my Daddy. He was a sweet man and his death created a painful void in my life."

Several weeks later Judi dreamed of her father. She remembers it not as a dream but moreover as an actual encounter.

Judi recalls the amazing experience. "He came to me in a large room or place, devoid of color or windows. It seemed to be a surreal space, one that was perhaps spiritual. He appeared as I had always remembered him, wearing his grey construction work shirt and pants. He sat me on his lap and told me how much he loved my brother and I and that he had not wanted to leave us. He explained that his parting was his life plan.

I melted into his arms as he embraced me, feeling his breath on my cheek, experiencing an incredible sense of peace and happiness. The time came for him to leave. Daddy assured me that I would not join him for a very long time, yet gave the promise of being together one day. He turned to smile and without another single word, vanished. Despite my young age, I recognized the experience to be a heavenly encounter, leaving me with a sense of profound love.

The same feeling of bliss comes to me each time I recall my father's appearance."

Many years later Judi had completed her nursing education. She was practicing as an RN on a psychiatric treatment unit in Rockford Illinois. It was at this time that Judi and I first met one another and became immediate friends. Our friendship has intensified and deepened over the past thirty years and our families and children are bonded in an enduring love for one another.

It was during these early years that Judi became aware of psychic energies. There is an intrinsic piece in psychiatric nursing that requires a knowledge of spirituality and mysticism, an accumulated skill when dealing with people. The suffering seen by mental health professionals is often so primal that healers call on the unseen and the unusual to bind emotional wounds. Nontraditional communication is the hallmark of psychiatric nursing.

Judi's second spiritual encounter presented in her twenties. She dreamed that she was riding in an open convertible. "I was sitting in the passenger seat and it was early in the morning, just after sunrise.

I was unable to see the driver but it seemed that he was a young male. His body was visible to me but his face was clouded in a foggy mist. He seemed unaware of my presence and we did not speak. He never looked over in my direction. Suddenly without reason or warning he accelerated the car and drove into the back of a large flatbed truck. The impact was thunderous and violent. It was terrifying. It seemed that the phantom driver drove into that truck, intentionally. Instantly I was out of the car and awake in my bed." Hours later Judi discovered that the son of a family friend had been killed that very morning at the very time of Judi's dream. He was traveling to have his third dialysis treatment that week.

The memory of the accident has never left Judi. The reason she was offered the experience remains a mystery.

As time passed, Judi became a wife and mother and continued to practice nursing. She was well intended in visiting her grandmother who was confused and suffering from Dementia. Judi's life had become very busy and the visits were mostly random. Earlier she had reviewed her grandmother's medication with the staff and oversaw her care.

One particular day Judi was devastated to find her grandmother over sedated and drooling. "I had terrible guilt. I should have been more involved, I was not aware of how she was suffering." Several weeks later, Judi's grandmother died. She dreamed of her grandmother. The dreams were painful, reliving the guilt over and over again. Judi was tormented.

Finally, two years later, Emma, Judi's grandmother visited her in a dream.

"Grandma brought me my favorite chocolate chip cookies. She wiped away my tears, held me and told me that she *was free now, happy and not suffering*. She repeated that her death and the circumstances around her death had not been my fault. She loved my guilt away. She rarely visits my dreams these days, only when I am distressed.

Her visits are a treasure and I can remember her now without the painful remorse."

Judi was now convinced that there is more to life than most people realize. Spiritually we remain connected to loved ones who leave their earthly existence.

When Judi's mother fell ill, Judi was living in Florida and her mother in Illinois. Judy recalls her mother. "My mother, Phyllis, grew up on a farm and was no stranger to hard work. She was self-sufficient at an early age. Growing up, I remember her large gardens, the canning and the cooking to feed us during the winter".

"My father spent much time at the VA hospital and Mother was essentially raising my brother and I alone. Despite her plight, I remember her delightful laughter. It sounded like tinkling bells and she would often laugh until she cried. She was a wonderful cook and people stood in line for her desserts".

Judy flew back and forth frequently. Her mother's illness was serious and her prognosis was guarded. She often stayed with friends for a port in the storm and emotional support. After seven harrowing months, Judi's mother succumbed to her illness.

"When my mother died I sadly realized that we would never again sip a cup of coffee together, never share recipes or long phone calls to one another. The thought was very painful, yet there was the funeral to plan and Mother's trust and will to deal with.

My personal grief would have to wait until the particulars were addressed."

Judi's husband Harvey began the journey from Florida to Illinois with their daughters, Rachel and Rebecca. Harvey had a special skill that of being psychic and what I describe as second sighted. Put simply, he is able to see spirit. It would be his responsibility to make the journey to Illinois, a twelve hundred mile distance in twenty four hours. He needed to join Judi to give her support and assist in planning the funeral service.

It can be a daunting endeavor, driving with no sleep and a deadline to meet. Staying alert and awake during this marathon would be a true challenge.

Two hundred miles behind him, Harvey became aware of a presence in the vehicle. The girls were both asleep in the back seat and there sat their grandmother between her two granddaughters! Harvey remembered that she looked well and happy. Her features were veiled and she seemed to be behind glass. She was unable to communicate verbally, so instead held up a sign that read *"Be Careful. You are tired. You must protect my granddaughters."*

Her message was clear and she remained in the vehicle the entire night, up to and including Harvey's stops for food and restroom breaks. Once in Rockford, the special traveler, now joined by a middle aged man, disappeared.

The funeral service was lovely. Judi had included her mother's favorite necklace, one of rubies and diamonds. It had been a gift to her from Judi and Harvey and the girls on what was to be her last Christmas. It had been her most precious possession and wearing it at her funeral had been a specific request by Phyllis.

Harvey was aware of a presence after the funeral, a vision of his mother-in law, searching under chairs and behind doors. She and her male comrade were seeking the expensive necklace and seemed distressed. Once she realized that the necklace was in safe keeping, she and the man who accompanied her faded into the shadows and disappeared. Harvey would later recognize the unidentified man as Judi's father, Edwin, whom he had never met.

Judi reminisces after her mother. "I see her in my dreams. The song *I'll Be There* was played at her funeral.

I hear the song occasionally, on the radio, in restaurants or in my dreams when I need to spend time with my mother.

I know she is with me, only a dream or vision away. It is my gift from beyond."

THE LOOKING GLASS

"IN THE MIRROR A REFLECTION OF
OUR YESTERDAYS, OUR TOMORROWS,
ETERNITY"

Kobler

Chapter 8

A PRECIOUS HEIRLOOM, the magnificent mahogany mirror hung reverently on the dining room wall. Massive and ornate, it had once belonged to her parents and was now a treasured remembrance. Their daughter faithfully polished it each and every Saturday, a loving act of reverence, believing that by some magic or miracle, they would one day see one another's reflection in the large looking glass.

The mirror had been placed strategically on the wall of honor, surrounded by adored family portraits, those of smiling brides and grooms and cherub faced grandchildren. Other faces, great grandparents and her own three children gazed back with beguiling smiles. The wall of portraits with the magnificent mirror, was a wondrous place indeed.

It was there in that gathering room that the holidays, family celebrations, birthday parties and festivities were always enjoyed and celebrated.

There in that room with its mystical mirror and echoes of family laughter, there would she wait patiently for her loving parent's reflection, envisioning and longing for their homecoming.

As the years passed, her hope never wavered. She lovingly and faithfully polished and tended the family mirror, adding ever more portraits to the wall, one by one as the family grew.

The happy family celebrated and enjoyed life until one very dark day arrived.

Sudden tragedy and the loss of their child was crippling in the anguish. The family had never endured such a trial and the grief cast a melancholy darkness over the beautiful mirrored wall with its enchanted smiles.

Now haunted with loss, the family struggled to reconcile their broken hearts.

Three years after the death of their child, the woman and her husband were awakened at 3 AM by a startling loud thud on the first floor of their house. They believed it to be a tree falling on their house, perhaps a car crashing through the walls. Instead, they rushed to discover that the magnificent mahogany mirror had crashed to the floor.

Amazingly, the mirror was undamaged but had come undone from the wall and fallen. All the treasured smiles remained safely in their appointed places on the wall.

The portrait of their son's children was untouched. A small figurine of three little birds had fractured into two pieces. Two birds on the right, the single bird on the left.

The woman knew this to be a visit from her mother, acknowledging the loss and separation of the woman's son, in fact her grandson. The broken figurine symbolized the separation and the unbroken mirror implied that they all endure, though apart, yet, together.

The magnificent mahogany mirror continues to adorn the dining room wall. She tenderly polishes and tends it each Saturday as she has for the past thirty years. The enchanted smiles and adored faces encircle it, each awaiting another mystical reflection and the next sacred homecoming.

ILLUMINATUS

"THE LIGHT OF GOD'S LOVE
WILL PIERCE EVEN THE
DARKEST NIGHT."

Anonymous

Chapter 9

THE SLEEPY LITTLE French village was charming, draped with fragrant red roses and honeysuckle tenaciously clinging to the ancient rock walls. Quaint houses nestled into the stone offered crooked surprises to the traveler on the twisting narrow cobbled streets.

The smell of bread baking teased the nose and tempted the appetite. In the distance someone played a melancholy tune on a violin. Small shops surrounded the plaza and beckoned wanderers. This enchanting place enticed, promising something unusual on that chilly November afternoon.

Deep in thought, the woman entered the small church. The chapel was not prominent, yet ornate in a simplicity that the woman found mesmerizing. A single large window decorated the altar, situated above the chapel, allowing anyone who prayed to kneel and also view the sky simultaneously. It had been no accident that this lovely little church had been created in this way to allow the faithful to envision Heaven as they kneeled to pray.

There must have been an inspiration that large miracles would emanate from humble hope in this sacred little church, this lovely *petite eglise*.

The woman's husband waited patiently for her outside the little French church. Having suffered the tragic loss of their child the year before, he was all too familiar with the flood of tears and the endless, desperate prayers ever since. Loving and supportive, he accepted that his wife could not pass this church without offering a prayer, not even now, on this visit to France and this inviting little French chapel.

They had planned this journey during their child's birthday. Having traveled all this way to escape the sorrow, they now realized that the tragedy had followed. Thousands of miles and the journey across the world would not offer the distance they sought. There would never be an escape from the loss.

Many of the others in the tour had wandered into little restaurants, sipping wine or delighting in a French croissant in the bakery. During the two week tour, these individuals had all become good friends with one another, possibly forging lifelong friendships.

Still, despite the invitations to join the others, he devotedly waited for his wife.

She kneeled at the altar. Remembering her child as an infant, a teenager and as an adult, she became overwhelmed. Crying out, she asked, "Lord why did you take my child from me?"

Ending her prayer, wiping away the tears, she looked upward to the window of Heaven and was stunned to see a brilliant blue light pouring onto her. The light was so overwhelming in its luminescence that she was nearly blinded in its radiance. Her husband entered the chapel at that very moment and realized that the prayer had been answered. They knew that they were no longer alone. The resplendent blue light was divine and in its sacred response comforted and calmed them. Heaven's window in the little French village had provided a miracle on that quiet November afternoon.

CLOUDS IN MY EYES

"Who are these that fly like clouds and like doves to their windows?"

Isaiah 60:8

Chapter 10

THE SOFT MELODIC tinkling awakened Karen and her daughter in the middle of the night. Heavy with sleep, Karen first thought it to be a dream, perhaps not real. The repeated urgings of her daughter, Melissa, however, quickly brought her to a complete state of awareness and wakefulness.

The haunting melody "Edelwiess" was emanating from the bedroom closet. Unsettled, alarmed and somewhat intrigued, Karen hesitantly investigated the mystical melody. In the closet played a fragile little music box, once given as a memento from Karen's mother-in law, no longer living, following a trip to Switzerland. The treasured memento had not been disturbed in many years and yet it played on with its tender musical serenade, bestowing a mystical message. Karen had no doubt that the visit was a loving one, that of the promise of love never ending, a reminder to always remember and to keep the thought of "Heaven's clouds" in one's eyes.

Born a twin, Karen and her sister happily shadowed one another into adulthood. Raised on a large farm, Karen Buttel Swinford knew the luxury of nature and the wealth of family.

Once an adult, Karen continued the close relationship with her family. Several years later, her father died. Karen and her mother became very close. Karen's mother, Rosetta Ross Buttell was a loving, caring woman who lovingly embraced all those who knew her, especially her children. Attending church together and actually living together for a period of time, the very close mother–daughter relationship deepened even more. "It was an enjoyable time, spending precious time with my sweet mother."

During this time period, Karen, a social worker became aware of a captivating poster at her place of employment. During her treatment plan meetings she became fixated on an inspirational poster in the large conference room. It was a cat, hanging by one paw on a line. The poster declared, *Hang in there, your faith will keep you strong.* "It seemed the poster was sending a message just for me. Several months later, following Mother's death, my twin sister was leafing through one of my family's bibles. We were stunned to find a clipping of the same poster in my mother's bible."

It was at that moment that Karen realized her mother's guidance had preceded her death, actually preparing her in advance.

Karen became aware of "knowings" shortly after her mother's death. She had been working in a retirement center. Upon her return to work, Karen studied the cat poster. It seemed a sign, as if to comfort her. She was speaking of her mother to her coworkers, reminiscing of how loving she had been, how she would miss her guidance and protection.

"My manager and I were discussing my mother's funeral, then two weeks past. It had been my first day back to work and I remained quite emotional." Karen suddenly began to notice small white cabbage moths flying all about the office.

It seemed very mystical and Karen inquired where the moths had come from?

Her manager responded that she had only noticed them once before in all the years she had worked at the office. The manager seemed intrigued as well.

Karen knew at that precise moment that the unusual visitors were a herald in announcing her mother's presence. "I knew that my mother was near, I could actually *feel her presence.*" Mesmerized, Karen proceeded to her car to make the journey home. As she approached her vehicle, she was startled by a large group of dark colored birds, hawking at her as if they were actually *speaking.* "It was as if they were, shouting a warning to me, as if they were actually calling out in unison an urgent warning." Shaken, Karen began the drive home with hesitation. Pensive and unsettled, she believed the warning to be an admonishment of pending danger or tragedy.

She believed that the unusual event was a continuation of the strange occurrences in the office earlier that day. Believing that she was being for warned, Karen became alert and hypervigilant.

She drove cautiously, slowly, as the hazardous, steep, road twisted and curved. Suddenly, a loud and grinding sound began in her front left tire. The car began to pull and steer violently out of control. Her heart pounded. She was terrified. The tire began to wobble, rolling off the axle as the vehicle began speeding towards the side of the road.

Miraculously, Karen, was able to steer the car to the shoulder of the road. Had it not been for the unusual premonitions, she might easily have been killed.

"My mother's spiritual visits on that memorable day actually saved my life. The miraculous experience has remained a wondrous gift to me and was the beginning of many more visits to come."

As time passed, Karen's children Sean and Melissa grew up, and married. Becoming a grandmother was a wonderful gift, with the promise once more of lullabies and story books. Her first grandchild, Payton, became the apple of her eye.

"I spent many happy hours with my wonderful grandson, he has since been a very large part of my life."

When Payton's father, Joel, became seriously ill four years later, the family rallied round one another, in an attempt to support each other and to protect precious, little Payton.

During the days of his father's illness, Payton began having thoughts and feelings about rainbows. Throughout the days prior to his father's parting, Payton began wanting rainbow ice cream. On several occasions, he requested rainbow ice cream.

Karen recalls.

"The day that Joel died, a rainbow appeared in the sky, one that was noticed by Payton." It seems that the rainbows had been a loving and tender communication from a father to his son.

Karen never loses sight of Heaven's clouds in her eyes. "It has become a part of life for me, a wonderful reminder that we never lose the ones we love."

CIRCLE OF ANGELS

"Be not forgetful to entertain strangers thereby some have entertained angels unaware."

Hebrews 13:2

Chapter 11

S AM BRINEZ ADORED his beloved grandmother, Raquel Naranjo. She had tenderly raised Sam from the age of five when the family had emigrated from Columbia to New York. "She was the most loving, caring and compassionate person I have ever known in my life. Grandmother was as if a second mother to me and others as well. She provided and cared for those less fortunate in sickness and in need. She was a spiritual woman, very religious and a strong believer in supernatural happenings. Having been raised by her for thirteen years, I became deeply spiritual as well. It was a loving gift passed on to me."

In 1995, at the age of 18, Sam moved from New York to Chicago Illinois. The parting was painful. He had accepted a position with the airlines and his future seemed bright and promising. Leaving New York was a necessary path to Sam's career, despite the sadness of leaving the family.

After Sam left New York, his grandmother fell very ill. So concerned, he began flying to her home on his days and week-ends off. Lovingly, he cared for her and took her to her physician appointments as often as he could.

For the last three months of her life, he was able to support her as she wished. She knew that he loved her and would have done anything for her. Sadly, his love could not save her."

Grandma Raquel passed away from cancer in 2005. Sam remembers that she often visits the family since her death. Sam's mother, Leyda, would often hear whispering voices in the house, her mother calling her name. The room becomes chilled, yet a feeling of love and peace permeates the rooms when it occurs. The family knows that the visits are a sacred gift.

Sam continued to work for the airlines while he attended college. He loved to travel and his position with the airlines made traveling convenient and very affordable. He and a good friend, Carlos, made the journey to Panama City. A break from school and work was a welcome respite.

One beautiful hot summer day, Sam and Carlos spent their time touring Panama City and exploring the various sites and tour attractions. They were so absorbed eating, laughing and talking, they lost track of time. "Suddenly, we became aware that we had wandered into a dangerous, desolate area. It had become very late, nearly four thirty in the morning. Dawn was approaching and we realized that we were hopelessly lost. We believed ourselves to be smart, cautious and experienced travelers, yet we had crossed a bridge and wandered into an impoverished area. Realizing that we were potentially in harm's way, we noticed two men staring at us. They began to approach us. Concerned that they would rob or attack us, I began to pray."

"I asked my friend to remain quiet as I was the only one of us who spoke Spanish. We became panicked, realizing that we seemed like helpless tourists. I began to pray to my Grandmother to protect us and bless us at this time of need. Suddenly, a beautiful small girl emerged from out of the bushes. She was stunning, dressed all in white with long dark shiny black hair.

She spoke to us in a soft, whispered voice, insisting that we turn around and walk in another direction. She admonished that we had arrived in an unsafe place. As she began to point out her direction, more and more children quietly emerged from the forest and began to surround us. There were as many as twelve children gathering about us in a circle and joining their hands as if to shield and shelter us from harm.

The two of us experienced an overwhelming sense of peace and safety as the circle of children gently guided us toward the main road. I knew then that the beautiful small girl was my grandmother, sweet and tender faced. Her loving spirit continues to protect me."

The two menacing individuals finally retreated. Miraculously, a taxi cab appeared which returned the two grateful travelers to the safety of their hotel.

Sam continues to feel the presence of his beloved grandmother. "At times she presents randomly, at others she visits when I am sad or longing for her. I will always treasure her loving ways and long for the day when we meet again."

Pennies from Heaven

"It was a small copper coin floating magically through the air, resting finally on my pillow. I knew it to be a gift from our brother, his promise that we are never parted."

The Brothers

Chapter 12

THE LEGEND OF the copper coin is ancient .The gift of a coin from spirit is the promise of abundance in the afterlife. The coin signifies something long lasting and as enduring as the human spirit. The mysticism of eternity is reflected in the immortal coin, a depiction of endless time and permanence. As indestructible as the human soul, it endures forever.

The tradition of leaving coins on military headstones dates back to the Roman Empire. The practice was also well noticed during the Viet Nam War. Comrades would leave a coin out of respect and as a symbolic payment for a toast upon their reunion.

While visiting some cemeteries you may notice that coins have been placed on graves by visitors. The coins have deep and distinct meanings when placed on the headstones of a   deceased soldier. The coin reveals that a visitor paid their respect to the fallen soldier. Leaving a penny commemorates the visit.

A nickel indicates that the visitor trained with the fallen soldier, a dime that the two served together and the quarter tells the family that you were with the deceased when he died.

It has long since been a tradition with the Jewish religion, to leave a small pebble, stone or coin atop a headstone to express prayers and the loving care and remembrance by the visitor.

The penny has also long since been recognized as the gift of the deceased to their loved ones who are left behind. The good fortune and loving representation of the penny implies the visiting spirit.

In ancient times, the coins were used to cover the eyes of the deceased and to offer payment and toll into the afterworld.

Once arrived in that resplendent place, the spirit offers the message of their safe arrival by returning the coins to their loved ones.

So goes the legend of pennies from Heaven.

The Kobler brothers, Matthew and Jason had suffered the tragic loss of their eldest brother, Jeremie in the fall of 2012.

His death had been sudden and tragic, caused by a motorcycle accident and had left them struggling with the overwhelming loss. The trio of brothers had been inseparable throughout their youth, a love for one another that continued into their adulthood.

Three souls navigated their childhood as if one entity, adventurous and incurable in their endless wanderlust. The fracture of the threesome left the brothers inconsolable. Despite the crippling grief, their family supported one another with strong faith and a formidable spiritual belief which offered them great hope.

The brothers knew that Jeremie would communicate to them, despite his death. They believed in spiritual life after death and had been raised enlightened. They had no doubt that he would contact them following his death. Though heartbroken, they were convinced that Jeremie would find his way back to them. Of this, they were absolutely certain.

A dream came at separate times to the brothers, that of a penny floating through the air and resting on their pillows.

So it came as no surprise when Matthew began to find pennies in the lint catcher of his clothes dryer. He later would find pennies on the seats of his car, airplane seats and his office chair at work. "Jeremie was assuring me that he was safe and I found it amazing and very reassuring."

Matthew was especially intrigued when photographs of his brother would tumble off the mantle spontaneously. The glass in the frame would never break, despite the noisy crashing to the floor. Afterwards, a penny would sit on the mantle in the vacant place.

"Photographs of my brother, Jeremie, would frequently tip over or fall to the floor without cause or explanation. I smile and immediately begin to search for a penny."

Jason, the youngest brother looked up to his big brother, Jeremie. "His death left a shadow of anguish on the entire family, such an overwhelming loss, yet we knew he would come to us in dreams and send signs to comfort and reassure us." Jason also began to find pennies immediately   following Jeremie's death.

Jason discovered pennies everywhere.   One afternoon, he was stunned when he found a penny lying on a leaf on the ground as he passed by.   Jason would discover pennies in the most unlikely of places.

Jason also experienced several dreams, Jeremie speaking to him, once encouraging his brother to *get out of bed and shave*. "It was very real, I got out of bed and actually began shaving. Then, laughing, I remembered what a prankster Jeremie has always been." Another was a   phone call in a dream, his brother calling him ...*I love you Beb....*"

The brothers continue to have spiritual experiences despite the passing of many years. The "Band of Brothers" remain united, forever, one world to another. Never parted, they remain interwoven, a semblance and shadow of one another, sharing not only blood, but spirit as well.

"THE GREATEST GIFT MY PARENTS EVER GAVE ME

WERE MY BROTHERS."

Author Unknown

THE PROPHECY

"FOR EVEN THE WISE CANNOT SEE ALL ENDS."

JRR Tolkien

Chapter 13

A WELL ACCLAIMED author, astrologer, hypnotist, therapist and speaker, Alice Stacionis is a most remarkable person.

Her adult life began in the nineteen sixties when, following high school, she studied to be a radiology technician. Disappointed when unable to find a position near her home, she began to seek other employment opportunities.

So intrigued by a posted position in Hawaii, working in a Chinese clinic, Alice immediately accepted the job. Her father offered his complete encouragement and approval. It would prove to be an experience that was life changing. Alice remembers, "Learning about other cultures would prove helpful in the future for me."

Three years later, Alice had been transformed by her time spent in Hawaii. She returned home, enlightened, exhilarated and ready for the next chapter in her life journey.

Alice spent five years working in a small community hospital and once more felt the call to change.

At this point in time, Alice began to study Astrology. She also accepted an HR position at a large manufacturing firm, one that employed four hundred employees. Alice was responsible for the safety, workers compensation and training of all employees.

The company was very supportive of their manager's involvement in various international programs and affiliations with ongoing education and training. Meeting with and securing professional speakers was an inspiration to her. "I learned so very much about people dynamics in various situations."

During this time, Alice met Dr. Bob H. and Dr. Stephen C. "One night at a company event, I made sure to sit at the table of the company owner. It was a bold move on my part as I really should not have been at that table. I knew it was meant to be. One of John's guests was Dr. Bob H., the former CEO of a local hospital and the consultant for John's many companies.

Dr. Bob was retired as a psychiatrist but continued to speak on the rise and fall of organizations based on brain dominance. We became fast friends, having coffee almost every week."

Dr. Bob became a mentor to Alice, encouraging her in all her endeavors.

Inspired by many amazing people in her life, Dr. Bob and Dr. Stephen C., including many successful authors, Alice sensed a need to explore her legacy.

Her focus into Astrology deepened and her wisdom and knowledge from her affiliations enriched her future.

Fifteen years passed and Alice achieved her place in life as a very successful astrologer and speaker. She completed another pilgrimage to Hawaii where she met one of the last of the 800 true, Hawaiians. This wonderful individual became Alice's spiritual mentor.

Alice smiles when she describes the "coincidences" in her life, with the implication that there are no coincidences in life rather that all things are, actually, "connections".

These connections brought her Dr. Bob, Dr. Stephen C., her Hawaiian mentor and all the remarkable people who had mystically entered her life. Little did she realize that the best was yet to come.

In 2005, Dr. Bob's health took a turn. A week before his passing, he requested that Alice hypnotize him. "I tried to help him to be comfortable with his journey. We hugged and parted. It was within days that he passed."

The friendship was treasured by Alice and his passing saddened her. Despite the loss, she was grateful for having known him and for his guidance and friendship.

"Several days later, I was half napping, eyes closed yet awake. The day began with the promise of something *unusual.* I felt an increased sense of awareness, perhaps a feeling of expectation. As I rested, the air seemed electric. Dr. Bob's energy engulfed me. I envisioned his face although his face did not appear to me. I heard his voice although he never spoke. His presence was undeniable. I had never experienced anything like this before.

It was incredible. He communicated … *you have a book to write.* He knew that my response would be, *but Bob I'm not a writer….*

Within days I knew it was something I had to do."

Several days later, Alice's forty year old cousin also died. A few days passing, the cousin also appeared to her quietly and in the same manner. "She presented with a sense of urgency. "The cousin's message was *you have work to do.*

"I had never experienced anything like this before, or after, these spiritual appearances and messages. I knew that this was something I had to do."

The writing began.

Coincidences continued. An editor appeared in Alice's life. He was also a hypnotist. Later a psychic entered her life in time to review her manuscript. All things came into mystical alignment.

Four years passed.

Alice knew that finding a publisher would be a challenge. Attending an event, Alice met Anita Meyer a published author. Anita had written <u>Primordial Language, In Search of the Holy Language and Beyond the Bible Code.</u>

She suggested that Alice send a copy of her book to her publisher. Within the week he agreed to publish her book.

Alice reminisces, "of course I had to dedicate my book The Journey to Now and Beyond to Dr. Bob. and Dr. Stephen C., like bookends, staunch supporters from the beginning. As the book was published, Dr. Stephen C. died. "The dots all connecting we traveled full circle."

In 2014, while attending a book signing at Barnes and Noble with several other authors, I met Alice and Anita.

"When I met Linda Kobler, I knew that we were meant to connect.

All things come full circle. Dr. Bob attended Linda and her husband's wedding decades ago. I witnessed the psychic medium deliver the message to Linda described in the first chapter of this book. We were destined to meet. I continue to long for more spiritual visits and experience amazing connections.

My continuous inspiration completes the prophecy."

DADDY'S VOICE

"THE HUMAN VOICE IS THE ORGAN OF THE SOUL"

Henry Wadsworth Longfellow

Chapter 14

H AVING SUFFERED MANY tragic losses, Judy Lamz Tilton never surrendered her faith or focus in life.

Her beginnings were challenging. Having been born prematurely, she spent much of her adult life reconciling issues with a congenital fusion of her neck and a multitude of related issues with her back. These ailments remain ongoing. Despite this, she perseveres. She jokes that she is made of "cement."

I believe that she is on earth as a healer, an earth bound angel in perpetual search of loving causes and other's needs to satisfy and accomplish. One rarely hears a complaint from her as she quietly continues on in her generous, altruistic, spiritual journey.

Having endured the loss of two wonderful husbands, loving parents and an adored nephew, her faith and belief in endless life has deepened. She is no stranger to grief and anguish. She is, however, a relentless believer in the beyond that waits for all of us at our parting.

Having been spiritually schooled by her parents, she is always vigilant of signs or messages from deceased loved ones. Her favorite quote from the bible? "For those who believe all things are possible." Mark 9:23. Judy remarks that this one quote is the core of her faith.

As a newborn infant, Judy fit snugly into her father's hand, much like a tiny doll. Weighing only three pounds and two ounces she seemed delicate and fragile. Tiny premature babies rarely survived in the late forties and early fifties. It has only been in the past two decades that NICU's have realized their amazing success in saving premature babies.

As a result, it would have been nearly impossible, several decades ago, that such a tiny infant would survive. The physicians declared her survival a miracle. Judy was heaven sent. Her mission had been ordained. That formidable, relentless little spirit was intended to be here, protected, perhaps, on a sacred level.

The photograph of her father holding his precious little daughter in his hand is very moving. From that point on throughout her life, Daddy called her "Baby."

Her age never mattered, he would always refer to her as "Baby." In her father's mind, she remained a tender treasure forever in his hand and in his heart.

As the years passed, Judy remained strong. One loss coupled by another, then yet another would shatter anyone's foundation. However, Judy has the spiritual and religious countenance to withstand, not unaffected, but moreover, faithful, pensive and patient, knowing that there is more to our stories than this earthly plane. She is a devout believer in "heaven hath in store what thou hath lost." In other words, time would reunite her with her loved ones. Of this she had no doubt.

She spent much of her life and money on her nephews, having no children of her own. There were no limits to her generosity. She assisted in funding their college educations, subsidizing and supporting their pursuits.

In league with their parents, she helped to make her nephew's every dream and hope come true.

An avid gardener, Judy has tended thousands of flowers over the years. She cares for her garden as she cares for loved ones...tenderly and with loving intention.

On any given summer day, one can find her planted somewhere out of doors transplanting, watering or clipping. Often referred to as "Mother Nature" by her appreciative neighbors, she can be found in her glorious garden pruning roses or trimming honeysuckle.

On one such day much like this, Judy had spent the early afternoon in her garden. She had been ill recently, having fallen and fracturing and dislocating her shoulder. The garden provided quiet sanctuary as her injuries reconciled. The healing was painfully slow and had taken much longer than imagined. The surgery had weakened and weathered her stamina. Judy was left with a shadow of melancholy and the "blues."

Angels can also bruise their wings.

On that warm summer day, Judy returned in doors. She prepared a cup of tea and a small lunch. As she relaxed, she noticed the red flashing light on her answering machine. She was perplexed.

She had taken the phone to the garden with her and did not recall the phone ringing. Why was the light flashing? Intrigued, she tapped the button.

"HI BABY" was the message.

It was clearly her father's voice. Stunned, she realized that following her illness and injuries, Daddy was compelled to comfort and reassure her from an ethereal place.

His miraculous voice is protected and preserved on tape. It remains tucked away in a precious place.

Once more, Judy was held in her father's hand and close to his heart.

ON THE WINGS OF A DOVE

The dove is an illuminati symbol of the Holy Spirit, that of sacrifice and rebirth.

Chapter 15

ELPIDIO ARTUS WAS born in Samar Philippines in 1962. One of eight children, life was challenging. So many mouths to feed and few resources required the Artus children to work very hard. A traditional childhood of light heartedness and play seemed a mere dream for those more fortunate, not for Elpidio and his siblings. Each child worked, selling food and clothing at the market places and on the streets. Before and after school, the children sold their wares. There was no time to play ball or have fun with friends. Faith and family comprised Elpidio's entire world.

Elpidio's parents were devout Catholics. Ernesto, his father, was employed by the Philippine army. Marciana was a housewife and a seamstress. Elpidio remembers, "Our lives were consumed with making it from one day to the next. There was little time for pleasures."

Marciana had dreamed of being a nurse all of her life, however the cost of education prohibited her from attending school.

Tender and caring, she was well known for taking in the sick and dying into their family home, for no pay and purely out of the goodness of her heart. Often these individuals were alone or had no family. She cared for those with contagious diseases, unafraid, because she was assured that GOD would protect her family. Her mission was that of caring for others less fortunate.

She was remembered for applying healing herbs on wounds, bathing and feeding and praying for the sick, often continuing prayers after their deaths. She would care for others until they drew their last breath, then pray over them to give their soul flight and a safe journey to paradise.

The prayers for the deceased would often continue for several days. The host or family members would then prepare food for all the guests. If the deceased had no relatives, Marciana would humbly share what little she had. She was so intensely spiritual that one of the relatives she had cared for appeared to her after the funeral in the same clothing she had been buried in. Marciana considered the visit a precious gift. Elpidio loved her deeply, "my mother had a heart of gold and was loved by everyone."

At the age of twelve Ernesto, Elpidio's father, died. The children were quite young and the loss of their father proved devastating to the family. Raising the children alone, paired with the overwhelming grief had proved insurmountable. Marciana loved her husband so deeply that she died one year later of a broken heart.

Realizing that they were without parents, the Artus children had to protect and comfort one another. It was a terrible and tragic time.

Elpidio, then age thirteen, reminisces about the miraculous funeral day, "we had all gathered at the cemetery where my mother was to be buried. The day was hot and sunny. I stood silently, weeping, regarding the tragic loss of my mother. Quietly, a beautiful dove began to hover above my mother's grave.

It flew, circling, as if in a spiritual dance or ritual. After a few moments, the dove perched softly on my right shoulder. It remained there for several long, amazing minutes. I stood completely still as if any motion would end the miracle. The sacred visitor brought me wonderful, loving, comfort. A voice from the crowd remarked that I would be the one to do great things for the family."

The encounter was interpreted by the people attending the funeral as the appointing of a "chosen one", the child that would in fact, provide for the family. Elpidio had no doubt that the dove had been a spiritual gift of strength from his mother.

Life for the Artus children became progressively more difficult. Now orphaned, the children began to work all the harder. Elpidio remembers going to school without food, "one had to make sacrifices."

The years passed and the children grew. An entity unto themselves, they persevered. Dedicated and reliant upon each other, the Artus children flourished.

Once grown, Elpidio attended school in the Philippines. He recalls the hardship of working and going to college full time. At the age of twenty three he made the journey to the United States where he was sponsored by a nursing agency to work at a medical facility as a registered nurse.

This opportunity, although challenging, allowed him to become an American citizen while he supported and provided for his siblings at home.

His sacrifice and altruism had been well rewarded. The spiritual visit from his mother had given him the courage and inspiration to indeed be the "chosen one".

DREAM WALKER

"Yesterday is but today's memory, tomorrow is today's dream."

KAHIL GIBRAN

Chapter 16

STAR REALIZED THAT her perpetual dreams were a message, perhaps a premonition of events to come. She began having the dreams two years after the death of her great grandmother, Katarina, and decided that perhaps the dreams were a spiritual communication from her. Great Grandmother had been second sighted and promised to be always near Star, protecting and guiding her. Death, it seemed, had not changed that loving promise. Katarina's love and protection continued from some celestial place.

Star's Yugoslavian roots endowed her with a rich mystical history and background and an inherent regard for dreams and signs. She realized that these messages were in fact *inside out gifts,* often revealing the dark along with the light. Revered and valued, Star paid close attention to these bestowals.

A recurrent dream was that of a ferocious wolf chasing she, her siblings and a beloved male cousin named Sasha. The dream always occurred in her small village and involved children running for their lives, jumping over the gate and fence to escape the predator.

In every dream all the children survived except for Sasha who was always attacked and killed by the vicious animal.

Star would wake with a violent jerk, heart pounding, palms sweating, screaming and calling out Sasha's name. Her largest worry was that the dream was intended as an admonition of tragedy for Sasha.

Great Grandma Katarina was sending her message of warning, not only to Star but to Sasha as well.

Fear engulfed her.

Sasha was a childhood playmate, in actuality, her cousin. They shared both blood and friendship. The same age, they were nearly brother and sister, always protecting and speaking for one another. The two of them against the world, their devotion never wavered. As they grew and matured, the bond remained unchanged. The childhood love for one another continued into their adulthood.

Night came once more and Star dreamed of a snowy mist, suffocating everyone in the village. Star and Sasha began to flee, racing for the gate. Sasha never reached the safety of the gate. The mist swallowed him.

Amazingly, Star and Sasha shared similar dreams. They believed that the time would come when the frightening dreams would eventually enter the light of day, affecting their very lives. They realized that the dreams were a premonition from Katarina, their great grandmother. They were ever vigilant.

Winters came and they went.

The dreams continued.

Great grandmother Katarina presented in Star's dreams, blowing kisses and sending omens of caution.

Star married and began a family.

Many years later, one frigid winter afternoon, a snow storm began in the small village. It was not an ordinary blizzard but one of epic proportion. The snow fell heavily, rapidly burying all things beneath. Schools sent children home early and roads were closed.

The little village was isolated in a valley of crippling snow, the white frenzy spinning as if to erase the picturesque little village forever.

Sasha had spent the afternoon working in an out building on his farm. The building was old and the roof was in sore need of repair. The weight of the heavy snow, blowing about with its wicked grasp, began to break the rafters.

Sasha rushed for the gate as he heard the first rafter moan. The roof buckled and instantly began to splinter. An escape was not meant to be. The roof violently collapsed upon Sasha. Suffocated by the snow and wounded by the rafters, Sasha died a few feet from the gate.

The admonition of the dreams had taken on light and their prophecy was tragically complete.

The neighbors would later reminisce that a wolf was heard, howling in the distant forest.

Star's eighteen years of dreams of the wolf, the gate and the poisonous white mist would finally cease.

Today she dreams sweet dreams of Sasha, his smiling face reassuring her that he is safe and well and with their great grandmother, Katarina.

Now finally able to rest, the dream walker drifts off to quiet, peaceful sleep.

RETURN TO ME

"RETURN TO ME OH MY LOVE I'M SO LONELY WON'T YOU PLEASE HURRY HOME TO MY HEART.

RETORNA ME CARA MIA TI AMO SOLO TU SOLO TU SOLO TU MIO CUORE."

Song Return to Me

Chapter 17

ELIZENDA WAS THE apple of her parent's eyes. The family had suffered the loss of three children to illness. She remained the only living daughter. Her three brothers, Dago, Ernest and Johnny, were likewise, adoring of their sweet little Eli.

She was dedicated to her faith. As a young child, she would play the organ at her family church. Never missing mass, Eli was deeply spiritual. She has always felt GOD near to her.

Early in her life, Eli became aware of her mother, Joaquina's, spiritual gifts. Repeatedly, her mother would have predictive dreams and revealed a second sight that the family attributed to her devout faith. Joaquina believed it to be GOD sent. Schooled in this belief, Eli witnessed and believed in spiritual vision as a child. This dedication continued into her adult life. Elizenda smiles and remarks, "my belief in miracles is a part of who I am."

Time passing, Eli grew up, married and became a mother Following her father's death, she insisted that her mother live with Eli and her family. There, she could care for and dote over her sweet mother.

Devoted to one another, Elizenda and her mother had lovingly shadowed one another throughout their lives. The sudden illness of Joaquina and her subsequent hospitalization in 1973 resulted in a first parting.

On that sweltering July day, Elizenda took her mother to the hospital. For the next several days, she stood vigil. Her mother repeatedly encouraged Eli to go home and rest, that she was feeling stronger and had finally begun to eat again. Her mother pleading, Eli reluctantly agreed. The last thing she wanted was to upset her mother.

As she drove home, an unexplained sense of sorrow overcame her. Tears filled her eyes. Wiping the tears away, Eli reconciled the mood to her fatigue.

Once home, she kicked off her shoes and prepared for a nap. Her respite and solitude was short lived. The alarm and terror of the phone ringing startled her, beckoning with the dark promise of tragic news. The hospital staff announced that her mother had died shortly after Eli's departure.

The dark clouds of grief engulfed her.

As the months passed, Elizenda remained guilt ridden. Perhaps if she had remained at the hospital her mother would yet be alive. Her mother dying seemed a tragic price to pay for leaving the hospital. Would her life ever be happy again? She was beguiled with the guilt of loss, waiting and hoping for a sign from her mother that she was forgiven.

The months passed painfully and slowly without the peace that Elizenda longed for.

The journey of birth and death remains one we are all destined to make on our own. Perhaps we are tenderly guided at the hour of birth by divine influence, protecting us from the duress. As with birth, death and our parting remains a sacred mystery, the true reveal of it undisclosed.

Are we then to leave this world and enter the other without trauma and desolation, accompanied by a divine intervention and no longer in need of human contact? Perhaps so. Death is as personal as birth, sacred and miraculous in its mystery.

One night Eli's long awaited patience was rewarded as she slept. "I dreamed that I was at the foot of a high mountain which I began to climb by crawling on my knees. I knew that my mother was at the peak of the mountain and I crawled for many hours until I finally reached her. She lovingly embraced me and we both wept with joy at our reunion. Not a word was spoken but my mother communicated to me *stop punishing yourself my love, there is nothing to forgive, you did nothing wrong.* This amazing encounter has remained with me since and has offered me great peace."

Eli's ability to communicate spiritually has continued with time. She planned to attend Lianor, her sister-in law's funeral many years later. Elizenda was anxious and nervous about flying to the funeral.

Despite the comfort of her husband, Edward, she was uncomfortable about the flight. While standing in their driveway, a vision of Maria, her sister in law who was deceased, appeared to her. "At that same moment, a beautiful butterfly appeared and encircled Edward, my husband and I. It fluttered about us, finally resting on Edward's shoulder where it remained for quite some time. As it departed, it encircled us once more and then vanished. I realized that this was a small miracle to calm and reassure me. We then proceeded safely on our journey to the funeral."

One night as Eli and Edward tucked into bed, a collection of several portraits on the wall behind them fell to the floor. The photographs were those of loved ones. "The painting of Jesus remained on the wall.

We knew that our loved ones had visited us that very night in a very spiritual way. They wanted us to know that they remain with us, loving us from a heavenly place and always vigilant over us. We were amazed and very grateful for their brief return."

Elizenda remains a dedicated believer in the spiritual presence of her loved ones. She continues to dream of her mother and those no longer with her. "I often stand in my kitchen with my back to the door and feel the presence of spirit approaching me. I expect to be embraced and then sadly, the moment passes. Without question I am surrounded by my loved ones, both alive and deceased. As I have always known, love is eternal. If only for a sweet moment, my loved ones return to me."

The Memory Box

"If I HAD A BOX JUST FOR WISHES AND DREAMS THAT WOULD NEVER COME TRUE, THE BOX WOULD BE EMPTY EXCEPT FOR THE MEMORY OF HOW THEY WERE ANSWERED BY YOU."

Jim Croce

Chapter 18

PATRICIA FELL IN love with Joe one warm summer night during a neighborhood volleyball game. Joe had been dating Patricia's good friend Mary. However, even Mary realized the immediate magnetism when the two met. From the moment their eyes locked the fireworks began. Patricia remembers the night, laughing. She describes the scenario, "I felt pretty guilty but all of our friends began to see that Joe and I were meant for one another. It was meant to be, sorry Mary."

The year was 1966 and the United States was heavily involved in the Viet Nam War. Nearly ten million young men were called to military duty. Joe was drafted to the US Army and received orders to deploy to Munich Germany immediately following boot camp.

Needless to say, parting was painful for the two young sweethearts and made a strong case for the truism that absence makes the heart grow fonder. The twelve months of separation passed very slowly and the longing to see one another grew.

Patricia was euphoric when a special letter arrived one day. Joe had written a sweet, romantic letter of proposal, asking Patricia to be his bride. There would be a lovely wedding upon Joe's return from Munich.

Wedding bells finally rang on January 13th, 1968. The newlyweds built a comfortable life for themselves.

Patricia was a registered nurse in the recovery room and Joe was a real estate broker. They welcomed their son, Daniel, two years later. The family circle was complete.

After a long and happy marriage the couple achieved community and business success. Happily, they raised their son, Danny, encompassing all the wonderful family vacations, sports games and special moments of parenthood. All their dreams realized, life was beautiful.

The clock ticked away the years. Danny grew up.

One unforgettable evening, Joe returned home from work. It had been an endless, demanding and exhausting day. He was fatigued in a way he had never experienced before.

Calling it a day, he quietly retired to bed. Lights out, peaceful slumber ensued. Joe would never awaken again.

Joe had suffered a heart attack. His family was heartbroken. His death had been sudden with no time to say goodbye, to offer words of love. The parting came quietly during the night and rendered painful finality.

I believe that in a spiritual way, humans remain connected. As lovers, parents and children, we develop a permanence with one another. Death is a temporary parting, as the tree dies in winter, only to resurrect in the spring.

Once created, energy never dies, it is in fact, eternal. Our bond to one another remains, though parted, together. Our nexus, though distant, is always near.

As the months passed, Patricia sold the family home. Danny was grown and living on his own. Living in the house alone seemed to be overwhelming. It was too large and downsizing proved to be the solution. She would be able to simplify her life.

After closing on the sale of the house, Patricia began having dreams, mystical encounters with Joe. Initially, the dreams were vague and fogged. She was able to hear Joe's voice yet was unable to visualize his face. Progressively, the dreams became clearer as did his voice and his presence. His message became distinct and more emphatic with each progressive encounter. Joe repeatedly pleaded with Patricia to "find the box in the attic."

Patricia was perplexed. The family house now sold, she had purchased an apartment complex with no attic area for storage.

She had no recall of a box of any kind when she had moved. What could Joe be referring to? It was truly a mystery.

The dream encounters became so frequent and fervent that Patricia would notice Joe's side of the bed disturbed, as if he had been sitting on the edge of the bed or lying there during the night. This was validation to Patricia that the encounters were very much *real*.

Studying the content of the dreams, Patricia speculated about the meaning. The next encounter came several nights later. The visit was so vivid and tender, Pat describes it, "I could feel Joe's arms about me and his kiss on my cheek. I truly felt Joe in the room with me. Then he whispered, that if I looked carefully I would find the box of which he spoke." *You must find it.*

Suddenly startled and awakened by the piercing ring of the phone. Patricia answered the call. It was her son Danny. It seemed that he had received a call from the new owners of their family home. They had discovered an amazing box in the attic, abundant with never seen family photographs, baby curls and teeth, ribbons and memorabilia. It was a treasure, a memory box, a time piece from Joe.

The mystery finally solved, the precious box was discovered and happily returned to the family.

Daniel and Patricia enjoyed a sentimental afternoon browsing through the wonderful items in the box.

Patricia continues to receive dream encounters from her husband. Joe no longer speaks of the box. He seems contented with the fact that the precious belongings are once more in the hands of his loved ones.

SECRET GARDEN

"AND THE SACRED BIRD FLEW ONE MILLION MILES TO CARRY MY LOVE HOME TO YOU."

Kobler

Chapter 19

HISTORICALLY, THERE has always been a religious appointment to the red cardinal. The beautiful bird has long been a symbol of the Holy Spirit. It is said that the Holy Spirit is depicted by two elements, one white light and the other, red flames. A dove represents the purity and white light of the spirit and the red cardinal represents the fire and vitality of the *living* spirit.

The cardinal represents the living blood of Christ and in the Christian belief, the life of the spirit is everlasting and never ending. In essence, the red cardinal symbolizes the renascence, of life, hope and restoration.

The message of the extraordinary crimson bird is that it brings the message of living faith and it reminds us that when all things seems dark or bleak, there is always hope.

Cardinal is also rooted in the Latin word for heart, *cordium.* A hinge or *cardo,* which allows the door of the heart to swing open, always moving and open to the spirit.

The oldest base root of the word Cardinal actually refers to the word cross. An ancient Norse word *kross* and the Latin word *crux* is interpreted as meaning a crossroad with a source of direction for those who travel the road of life…inferring that GOD is the guidepost.

The cardinal is a spiritual, mystical and religious bird that offers solace and guidance to the life traveler who may be anguished or has perhaps lost his way.

Following the death of our son, Jeremie in 2012, my physician called to tell me of an amazing encounter with my son three days after his death. The Dr. told me that Jeremie had presented during the physician's prayer time. My son appeared as a red cardinal, tapping on the window and taking human form once inside the Dr.'s home. Jeremie spent much time there, asking the Dr. to assure the family and his children that he was safe and in GOD's safe keeping. He appeared twice to the Doctor, both visits at the time of his prayers. The visits have since ceased.

Following the visits to Dr. Hussain, a red cardinal has frequented an area in our yard, referred to by my grandchildren as "The Secret Garden."

The visits are random, yet seem to occur at moments of my personal longing, the times I am most distressed about the loss of my son. I then feel a "beckoning" to approach the windows or to enter the garden. Without exception, the red cardinal presents at these times of yearning and imparts sacred sanctuary to me.

On June 14th, 2015, I spent the afternoon reminiscing about my children and felt saddened about the tragic loss of my Jeremie. As I drove into the driveway, the red cardinal swooped down over my car, fluttering into the nearby trees.

It remained there in the garden and continued to perch near the windows in the den. Once in the house, my tender guardian remained, assuring me that my son is always near.

Two weeks later, as I played with Jeremie's three year old twins, a majestic red cardinal flew into their yard. It perched quietly on a small bush near the deck. For several endless seconds, the mystical bird offered peace and repose to the three of us, who watch and wait every day for a sign and a message from my son and their Daddy so very far away.

In regal silence, love message delivered, the magnificent messenger flew away. Once settled in a nearby tree, it sang its whistling, haunting serenade and vanished.

On July 6th, my husband David's birthday, I was writing this chapter of the book. As I wrote, the red cardinal flew past the windows in the Secret Garden many times. It appeared excited and jubilant, racing repeatedly in frenzied flight. Often looking into the windows, as if it was aware of my presence, the cardinal finally perched on the window directly in front of me. Pensive, it remained for many seconds, in quiet repose. The amazing bird and I were so close, I could nearly see the beating of its heart. Whistling out its sacred message, the magnificent crimson cardinal flew away.

One week before the anniversary of Jeremie's death, I was standing in the secret garden. Raphael, a gentleman who prunes and cares for our trees stood with me. Without notice, the magnificent red cardinal flew between us, gently brushing my face with its wing. Raphael remarked that he had never had such an experience in all his years of working with nature.

He smiled and agreed that the visit had been a wondrous, sacred gift.

The cardinal continues to appear frequently in the garden. The lovely bird bequeaths its message of hope with every splendid visit.

The Dancer

"SO THE DARKNESS SHALL BE THE LIGHT
AND THE STILLNESS THE DANCING."

TS Eliot

Chapter 20

A LOVING WIFE, MOTHER and grandmother, Joann brought a zest for life to those around her. Her children especially enjoyed her tender devotion and adoration. She brought a loving light to her family and enjoyed a variety of interests and hobbies. However, all things considered, Joann had a special passion for dancing. She most loved disco dancing and had a wonderful sense of rhythm. Her daughter Barbara Martinez reminisces" watching my mother dance was like watching magic. She was her happiest when dancing, wearing her beautiful copper colored Disco dress and matching high heels. It was a sight to behold as she seemed to float across the dance floor. She was so beautiful and that wonderful image is forever imprinted in my memory."

Barbara's mother had been spiritually aware throughout her lifetime and shared those beliefs with her children. She saw the beauty and the joy in life and believed in those things unseen and unexplained.

Barbara was beguiled with the mystical stories of her mother, convincing her of life after death. Unafraid of death, she was assured that life is endless and death only a transition.

This education served as a comfort to Joann's children in a universal way. There was the promised hope and belief that love is eternal and that the parting at death is simply a changing from one realm to another.

Joann Zane-Minutilli-Dill died on September 15th, 2008. She was her daughter's "best friend, confidant, loving sweet mother and my heart and soul."

It was a few months later when Joann began her spiritual visits. Barbara would often awaken to the knowledge of having spent the night with her mother. "We would spend the night sipping coffee, laughing and sharing precious time, just as we always had. Our souls in a dream state, we were able to bridge the gap from one world to another, it was so amazing."

Barbara remembers that her mother was very devoted to her grandchildren. "She especially followed after my daughter Natalie. Mother loved all the frilly girly things and the two of them were very close .Our family had a coffee mug in the kitchen with a devil on it. In one spiritual encounter my mother warned not to let Natalie drink from the naughty cup (in reference to the mug). Happily, it kept our daughter on the best path".

Disconcerting, many months passed without any dreams or contact. Barbara worried that the visits may have ended, "Mother was my heart and soul, the two of us intertwined in a mystical way. The communication was so important and comforting to me that the end of it would have been heartbreaking."

"My mother presented in the dream as much younger, perhaps thirty five. She was so beautiful. She was smiling and laughing .She told me to tell my stepfather, Brian, her love of twenty-seven years, that he would not join her for a very long time.

Mother smiled with her mischievous smile and remarked that she needed more time to do *her own thing*. She continues with her incorrigible sense of humor, even in that other realm."

A few weeks later, while Barbara was relaxing and dozing in the sunshine, she became aware of a presence. Her eyes closed, her mother ran towards her. Suddenly Barbara felt her mother at her side. She was wearing a beautiful strapless blue dress, Hawaiian and flowered. "Mother kneeled at my side. I was afraid to move or breathe or even open my eyes for fear she might vanish. She spoke to me, calling out *Natalie, Natalie*...the name of my daughter. In the background stood a man with his back to me. It seemed that he was of Mexican descent, wearing a white cowboy hat, jeans and a flannel shirt. He was striking in that he had a long grey braid. I never recall ever meeting the man before, yet it appeared that he was very loving and protective of my mother. My mother then turned around, walked towards the stranger, with arms around one another and vanished".

The mystery unfolded months later when Barbara's sister shared a similar vision. "She also viewed Mother with the Mexican man. The two of them were seated side by side on a large stone bench. The unusual man was noted to have large, weathered hands as those of someone who had spent many years at hard work and toil. He was quite extraordinary and it appeared that our mother loved him very much.

The two of them presented with arms around the other's shoulder. The description confirmed that this was the same man in my vision on that warm summer day.

Following many reflective conversations with her husband, Barbara concluded that the man in the vision was her mother's spiritual guide.

"He seemed to accompany her on all her earthly visits, perhaps to prevent her from becoming lost, to assist her also in her return to the spiritual world. He appeared caring and protective of her, perhaps supportive and empathetic in her need to return to earth to communicate with her loved ones."

Barbara's husband remains devoted to his mother in law, Joann, and also experiences dreams and visions from her.

As we discover with age and wisdom, love is enduring and eternal.

"I consider my mother's beliefs a gift in my life. Of all the wonderful things offered me by my mother, these beliefs that life goes on after death is the most comforting and inspirational."

"Mother continues to appear to us from time to time, each time appearing more serene. She seems more detached, assured that we are well and have learned   her miraculous lesson. She is now more drawn to her new existence, perhaps exchanging her dancing dress for a silken robe.

One day I will reunite with Mother and that missing piece of my heart will finally be returned to me. As the sweet music plays *the two of us will simply dance away.*"

THE FAITH OF EMILY

IN OUR DARKEST MOMENT, THERE IS A LIGHT
WITHIN US WAITING FOR THE RIGHT TIME TO
SHINE AND GUIDE OUR WAY."

Dota

Chapter 21

SHE HAD REMARKABLY been named Emily Faith. Despite her tragic unfortunate beginnings, the beautiful name had been predictive of her exceptional and tumultuous life. As she would often would say, "My faith has never failed me. It has been the one thing that I could always rely on."

As a small child she had been abandoned by her natural parents. Once in the social system she had the misfortune of being placed with foster parents who later adopted Emily. Her circumstances did not improve, in fact, they sadly worsened. The little girl learned to make herself small and invisible in the shadows. She learned to stay out of the way. Despite her earnest endeavors, she suffered through a childhood of neglect and abuse.

Her life of challenge lead Emily to residing in a nursing care facility at a young age. Battling overwhelming physical challenges and long suffering, she had never abandoned her faith in GOD. It remained the one constant in her life, the only real protection she required.

As a small child, she had persevered through tragic emotional turmoil and trauma.

The scars of neglect and traumatic memories rendered a dark shadow over her life. When life became the most painful, Emily Faith relied on her belief in GOD. "It was my faith that kept me alive, it was all I had and it saved my life."

Plagued with the inability to walk or live independently without assistance, she perseveres and fights the good fight every day. Often in severe pain, she overlooks it and smiles, "everyone suffers, I am given no more than I can bear."

Now, years later at the age of forty five, she is pensive and wise, always sharing a quote from the bible or an inspirational remark to everyone in her path. She spends her days reading, writing and creating beautiful needlepoint works. She spends the entire year needlepointing Christmas gifts to bestow during the Holidays. Her favorite passion is offering grace at each meal in the nursing facility where she resides. Both residents and staff alike are mesmerized by Emily, her enthusiasm and zeal for life overflowing and resplendent.

She is a religious, spiritual and mystical enigma. It seems that while in her presence, she imparts a sacred sense that permeates the room.

One day as I visited, Emily Faith shared a most miraculous experience. She told me of one night when she was very ill and had awakened to feel the presence of someone in the room. "I felt the hands on my hands and a quiet voice that reassured me that I would never be alone, that HE was with me at all times, whether awake or asleep. I knew it to be the hands and voice of Jesus."

Emily Faith had never shared the beautiful experience with the facility staff. Fearing that others would dismiss it as a dream or hallucination, she kept her secret. "I would often feel a sacred presence in my room, I felt great comfort and happiness. I didn't want anyone to take my joy away."

Quietly, over the years, Emily Faith guarded her miracle, keeping it close to her heart. I felt honored to be the one she trusted to share the experience with. The miraculous visit continues to inspire the very strength that gets her through each day. I consider her amazing encounter to be a gift to me as well.

Looking back, I believe that there could have been no one more worthy of the miraculous experience. Emily Faith has suffered enormously, and yet, beyond all odds, relied on her strong faith to persevere.

Despite her anguish, she revels in every milestone and appreciates every gift in life, no matter how small. She regards others with a genuine interest and tender caring. Emily Faith is a remarkable, unforgettable person.

As I left her one evening following a late visit, I assured her that not all voices and visions are delusions, that in fact, I believe that she had witnessed the divine. She nodded, kissed my hands and, smiling, drifted off to peaceful sleep.

THE FLIGHT OF BUTTERFLIES

JUST WHEN THE CATERPILLAR THOUGHT THE WORLD WAS OVER, IT BECAME A BUTTERFLY

Proverb

Chapter 22

PATRICIA DACE HAS always believed in "spirit", that part of us that continues after death. She cannot remember when those beliefs came upon her, "as a child I suppose, but I have always felt that our lives go on after death. It is a wonderful promise to me."

She was raised in a large Polish-Swedish American family. She remembers family gatherings with her grandparents and all the cousins, food and festivities.

Pat grew up in life quite abruptly. Her mother was often ill and being the oldest of four children, acted as a mother surrogate to her siblings. She has a warm and nurturing presence and her sisters treasured her as a part time mother and caretaker. The sisters remain close and involved with each other today as a result of their remarkable childhood.

As a child, despite her responsibilities at home and school, she persevered. She recalls many trials throughout her life.

Without fail, a butterfly would rest in her hair, or rest on her shoulder when the burdens seemed overwhelming. "It seemed they were mystically drawn to me."

"I am unsure of the visitor, but I believe it was intended as a gift to reassure and comfort me. The visits have occurred several times in my life, always at times of personal challenge."

Having suffered cancer, a difficult first marriage and raising a child alone, Pat withstood the storms and the tribulations. She refers to a favorite poem about a mighty oak tree, its roots buried deep in the ground and its ability to remain standing despite its bark being destroyed and its branches broken. "I would imagine the poem describes my life in a very accurate way."

Pat's patience and strength was rewarded when she met and married her second husband, Dave, twenty years later. They would embark into a wonderful marriage which today culminates to twenty one years. A loving support to one another, Pat finally achieved true happiness.

Tragedy never far away, Pat's wonderful sister Cindy died tragically in a house fire in 2001, a massive loss. The family suffered.

Following Cindy's death, Pat was visited once more by butterflies of vivid color and magnificent wings. Pat was assured that her sister was sending messages of love and hope.

Many years into their marriage, in May of 2015, Dave became gravely ill. Having been a wounded Navy veteran, he had fought his own battles in life. The old wounds resulted   in a life threatening illness, one his physicians and the family expected he would not survive.

Pat would call on her reserve once more. She would remember the mighty oak tree and cling to its shelter during this storm. Branches twisted, leaves scattering and wind blowing, she would pray.

Dave remained in a coma for two weeks. Critically ill, he was hospitalized at the VA hospital in Madison Wisconsin. Pat had spent the long hours at the hospital as she had done every day since his illness. Exhausted and spent, she began her journey home to Illinois only to return once again in the morning.

Having stopped for coffee, Pat sat quietly in the beautiful little park, eyes closed as she prayed and reviewed all the comments made by the medical staff. She envisioned her husband, asleep and very ill in his hospital bed. Would life ever return to normal for either of them and their family?

As she opened her eyes she was amazed to find a large, magnificently colored butterfly resting on her blouse beneath her chin.

A few people had gathered, mesmerized by the attention of the butterfly to Pat. Despite the strong wind, the lovely messenger remained for several minutes. Pat realized that the intention was spiritual, a voice of hope from a celestial place. Perhaps it was the herald of a miracle.

The next morning Dave opened his eyes and miraculously emerged from his coma.

The miracle had been realized.

THE MUSIC NEVER ENDS

"MUSIC EXPRESSES THAT WHICH CAN NOT BE PUT INTO WORDS AND CAN NOT REMAIN SILENT."

Victor Hugo

Chapter 23

A SOFT WIND BLEW his beloved lullaby through the starry night, tears sparkling in the air on that warm summer evening. It was a tender song, well remembered as the one his mother often sang as he drifted off to sleep. *Mocking Bird* had been his favorite lullaby from childhood. He had recalled it during illness as a child, as a comfort while a young man at war and last of all at his own moment of death.

He knew that his mother had been destroyed at his death. Unable to reconcile the loss, he often found her here, primping and prodding at his grave, arranging flowers and kissing the ground under which he now lay. At the very least, he could send her sweet melodies reminiscent of their time spent together, sweet music of the memories of mother and son. He would fill her heart with song and remind her that he was always near, and that as with enduring love, the music will never end.

He would often feel his father's heart calling him, longing for his return. His father wished only to hear his voice once more, one more embrace, so little to ask, yet never to be.

As comfort to his father, he would send the song *Green Beret* as a reminder of his dedication to the military during his young life. His father would know it to be a loving message. He would often hear it on the radio as he drove into the memorial garden. It was a small way to send love to his grieving father.

His siblings suffered with the anguish of grief, remembering times shared as children, rough housing, the secrets and tenderness of spending time together. Their brother's death had created a void in the world, an irreconcilable loss. They would dream of him, often awaking to the certainty that he had been there visiting with them during the night. Now, he would fill their ears and memories with his favorite song, *It's a Wonderful World* and they would know it to be a message meant just for the two of them.

To his beautiful children, he would send soft echoes of *You Are My Sunshine* and remind them of a sacred time when their Daddy held them in his arms. They would feel his love and know that he sends music as a soft kiss, dancing through the air as if by magic. The love for his little ones would transcend death.

The melodies danced rhythmically through heaven's skies, softly arriving on a radio to carry his sweet message home. He would send the music frequently so as to let his family regard it as a gift from him, to comfort and remind them that he longs for them as well.

As for him, the music will never end.

ALL THE WAY HOME

"AND SO THE BUTTERFLY, THE COLOR OF NIGHT, FLUTTERED TENDERLY ABOUT HER FACE, KNOWING THAT IT WAS FINALLY HOME."

Kobler

Chapter 24

RUTH ROY WAS born in Gujarat India. From the time of her birth, Ruth's family realized that she was unusually gregarious and vibrant. Her view of life as a child was inspirational, finding wonder and pleasure in all that she experienced. Filled with love and magic, her childhood was memorable.

Ruth recalls her youth, living on a large farm, "My grandfather was Portuguese and spent much time at our farm. He was great fun and very sweet and loving. He would drive us about on his motorcycle through the mango orchards, it was a wonderful time."

It took great sacrifice and courage to travel across the world, leaving her wonderful India and her loved ones behind her. Married with two young daughters, Ruth was the first of her family to leave her home land for the promise of America. The journey would be a challenge. The parting would inscribe a longing for her siblings and parents and render a life time love of her home so far away.

The years scattered and her beautiful India seemed a distant memory. The transition from one continent to another, though painful, was complete.

Raising her daughters and caring for her home and family, Ruth remained occupied and busy. Although content, her life and childhood in India called to her. India and her culture was engrained in her very being.

"I would often dream of eating fruit fresh off the tree and running in the orchards with my brothers and sisters. I would envision my mother watching out the window, calling her children to dinner or singing with her beautiful voice early in the morning. My parting from India was usually the theme of my dreams."

In September of 1983, Ruth's mother Vanita L. Daniel died suddenly. Anguished, she returned to India. Despite her frequent visits home over the years, the longing for her mother had never ceased.

As she entered her parent's home, Ruth was overwhelmed with a feeling of anticipation. It had been some long time since her last visit. Now, being home again on the anniversary of her mother's death was painful.

Ruth believed in her heart that somehow her mother would welcome her home and give her a "sign."

The sign would not come for twenty five years.

"I visited my parent's home in 2010. By that time, my uncle was living in our family home."

The anguish over her mother's death had never reconciled. Each time Ruth entered her parent's home, she became a child once more, a child who had been parted from her mother. The melancholy had remained, the longing for the days of sitting at her mother's knee.

Having waited all those many years for a communication from her mother, she had never surrendered hope. Standing in the doorway of her family home, a magnificent onyx colored butterfly began to flutter about her head and face. The mystifying dance continued for several amazing minutes.

Stunned, she knew immediately that the visitor was endorsed by her mother.

Mesmerized, Ruth's uncle remarked that he had *never* seen a black butterfly nor had he ever seen one in the house. Smiling and embracing Ruth, he declared that the beautiful butterfly was in fact a heavenly visit from her mother. Filled with tears and joy, Ruth finally had her celestial sign, the message she had waited for all these many years.

In many cultures, black butterflies are believed to represent metamorphosis. They depict transition, freedom and renewal but primarily, rebirth. The black butterfly is believed to be a sacred messenger, to comfort and offer hope to loved ones who remain on earth. They are legendary in Eastern cultures for appearing inside the home. The black color is associated with the powerful emotions such as sadness, mourning or loss of a loved one. Their manifestation is rare as they are elusive and are nearly always related to a spiritual visit.

In 2013 Ruth was watering her garden, bountiful and lush with vegetables and fruit. As her mother, she loved the soil and the raising of fresh food to share with family and neighbors. One sunny afternoon, the resplendent black butterfly returned.

Ruth was delighted when once again the magnificent visitor fluttered intimately and lovingly about her face.

In 2015 Ruth celebrated her birthday with family and friends. Her sister had lovingly given Ruth a birthday card, embellished with lovely butterflies. As they returned to the house from the patio, the black butterfly appeared once more, hovering about Ruth's face. "I knew now, finally, that my mother had come all the way home, all the way home to me."

TOGETHER AGAIN

"THE KEY TO MY HEART YOU HOLD IN YOUR HAND, NOW NOTHING ELSE MATTERS WE'RE TOGETHER AGAIN."

Buck Owens

Chapter 25

ALTHOUGH HER NAME was Mary, Eileen Brickley was always called Eileen. A devoted school teacher in her early twenties, she loved the demands of teaching in a one room school house. As a daily necessity, she started and stoked the fire to warm the little school. Time spent there was a challenge, seemingly a preparation for her future experiences in life.

Teaching was replaced soon after her marriage with the daily demands of a farmer's wife. Charles Ennis Brickley entered her life and Eileen happily became a loving wife and mother on their wonderful farm.

Eileen and Charles were wonderful business partners. As is often experienced by most farm wives, the responsibilities and chores are many. The management of the home and children, as well as book keeping and cooking for the family can be daunting. Up at dawn and off to bed late is the price of farm life.

Despite the challenges, Eileen and Charles prospered. The hard work was well rewarded with a successful business and a growing family of four children.

As the years hurried by, the family grew. The Brickley children had families of their own. Eileen and Charles retired from the farm and began a business in real estate. The new business required increased book keeping.

The family began to notice a tender affliction with their father. It was touching and always drew laughter.

It seemed that each and every time he was balancing the books, he was always off in the balance by ten cents.

Eileen would hunt with him, searching for the missing dime. After some time, the two would discover the mystery and the missing ten cents. They would shake their heads and laugh. It was a legend in the Brickley family.

Eileen lived many years following Charles's death.

She continued the business and the legend of the missing dime until her death at the age of eighty.

Mary Brickley, her daughter, suddenly began to notice dimes appearing in the strangest of places. "I found them under door mats, on furniture and in the washing machine. They would pop out at me everywhere I went! My sister has continued to have the same experiences as well. It is truly amazing. "

With tears in her eyes, Mary remarks that she knows the dimes to be a visit from her parents. Mary remarks that often when she visits her parent's graves, she often hears soft whispers of voices. She is comforted by the loving events.

The tender visits and coins assure her that Eileen and Charles are, in fact, "together again."

THE ANNIVERSARY

"I HAVE FOUND THE ONE WHOM

MY SOUL LOVES"

SONG OF SOLOMON 3:4

Chapter 26

H E DECIDED TO take a break after snow plowing since early that morning. An employee of Arlington Gardens, it was his responsibility to maintain the cemetery roads. Typically, the weather forecast had predicted two inches of snowfall despite the punishing reality of six. William Kocureck realized the expectation of all the loving caretakers who visit the gardens come rain shine or snow storms.

The snow continued to fall softly on hallowed ground.

Resting against his truck, he marveled at the beautiful snow covered acres of land, strategically checkered with the memorial monuments of deceased loved ones.

He was always touched by the daily visits from parents or children, husbands, wives and siblings tenderly grooming graves, all the time longing for the return of their loved ones.

The weather never seemed to stop the loving, steady flow of their devotion. He was often amazed at the continual traffic, the comings and goings of the families and visitors. They were well worth his extra effort.

As he was lost in thought, a gentle wind began that sent the snow flying about in a white whirlwind. It seemed unusual, this ethereal ballet of snowflakes, like nothing he had ever seen before. The breeze rested around an ancient grave, one there for many decades.

The flurried frenzy spun about in a hypnotic fog. William was stunned when he began to see through the fog two haunting figures embraced and dancing. At first he believed the mirage to be a result of the cold frigid air and the windy flurries. Taking a longer, closer look he was convinced that the elderly couple dancing in the snow around the grave were in fact, *real.*

The mystical waltz continued, the loving duo twirling and laughing, dancing around their grave as if time for a few precious minutes stood still. The couple holding the other in a tender embrace shared a long awaited kiss.

As suddenly as the magnificent encounter began, the wind stopped and the haunting dance ceased. The loving couple vanished.

William walked through the deep snow towards the amazing stone. He smiled as he discovered foot prints and the marks of dancing in the otherwise, undisturbed fresh fallen snow.

"It was an amazing day, one that will always stay here, in my heart."

William would later discover that the waltz occurred on the couple's eightieth wedding anniversary.

THE LETTER

"MORE THAN KISSES, LETTERS MINGLE SOULS."

John Donne

Chapter 27

H E REMEMBERED ALL the wonderful time spent with his grandfather. Counting stars, fishing and long walks in the woods remained a memorable part of his childhood. It wasn't that Jerry did not appreciate *all* of his family, it was simply the fact that there was something really special about his grandfather. Whenever Jerry entered the room, his grandfather would brighten, as if a hundred lights had been turned on. Jerry was truly the smile on his grandfather's face.

Needless to say, their time spent together was magical. Jerry loved to hear all the old stories and musings. Time stood still when they were together. The two were inseparable.

As often happens, however, the everyday demands of working and school can steal away precious hours. As Jerry grew, the visits became few and far between. It had been quite some time since Jerry had visited or called his grandfather.

Realizing that his grandfather had not been in the best of health, he decided one day to write a long letter to him. Jerry was certain that the letter would please his grandfather.

The ink danced across the paper, writing paragraphs of sweet memories of childhood, adding punctuations and periods to his hopes and dreams of the future. Hours later, the masterpiece complete, the document was lovingly sealed and stamped. Placed in the mailbox, the letter was absorbed into the hundreds of other postal pieces. Jerry would love to see his grandfather's face upon the opening. This would bring a smile to the grandfather's face, to be sure.

Jerry busied himself the rest of the week, attending school and addressing the myriad of functions with friends and schoolmates. The letter seemed a forgotten detail.

The announcement of his grandfather's death the next day burned the tears from Jerry's eyes with stabbing disbelief.

His heart stood still.

Jerry was heartbroken.

Understandably, a flurry of activity followed, the plans for service and calls to the family. Throughout the day, Jerry could think of nothing else except the letter.

Had his grandfather received and read the letter before his death? Did he know how much his grandson loved and revered him? The questions ran through Jerry's tortured thoughts.

Exhausted, Jerry fell into bed that night, eyes swollen from tears and his heart heavy from the loss and guilt. Perhaps sweet sleep would allow some sanctuary and escape from the long day of anguish. The letter was his last thought as he drifted off to rugged sleep.

A soft voice called Jerry out of his sleep. He felt the quiet pressure on the side of his bed as his grandfather sat next to him. Jerry could smell his grandfather's favorite aftershave.

Jerry embraced his grandfather and they wept.

By some appointed miracle or magic, his grandfather was actually *here with him, not a dream but actually here at his side.*

The visit assured Jerry that his letter had been received and was actually found in his grandfather's pocket after his death.

They spoke for several hours, the grandfather promising frequent visits. He smiled and thanked the grandson for the wondrous letter, admitting it was the finest gift he had ever received.

The visits continue several times a year.

Jerry now writes letters regularly to loved ones and close friends.

Love never dies.

IN YOUR DREAMS

THE LONGING FOR SACRED EMBRACE,

IF ONLY IN YOUR DREAMS.

Kobler

Chapter 28

H E WOULD NEVER forget the kissing of little toes and fingers and rocking his baby boys to sleep. One by one, as they entered the world, David adored his three sons. They would become his entire world, his wife and his boys would be the complete focus and dedication of his life.

As his sons grew, he assumed the role of being their greatest fan. T ball, scouts, school programs, football, art shows, music concerts and Rugby games would find Dad devotedly cheering somewhere in the audience. Without exception, David was a very proud and dedicated father.

His sons adored their father as well, loving apples falling very close to the parent tree. David smiling, recalls" our boys were always ready to kiss us hello and goodbye, never embarrassed to embrace us in a crowd or gathering. The love we give is the only thing in life that returns to us."

Each embrace was offered to the little boy who walked away the man."

College and military graduations captured the pride in his heart. Three fine young men emerged from the loving support and inspiration from their two loving parents. Still, the sons remained close to their roots, always finding time to spend with their adoring father. Family was their core. It was the grounding force.

Time passing found the sons grown men, beginning their own lives and leaving home. Parting was painful. Weddings, graduations and military deployments beckoned and their lives became focused on new horizons. Life called and the birds left the nest. Their flight rendered many sleepless nights.

David was pleased that his sons were content. Education and the sacrifice of military service filled his boy's lives. Phone calls, emails and short letters filled his days with their accomplishments, Dean's and President's list, book publishings and military honors were lavished on the wonderful sons.

Life was very sweet for David as he reveled in the success of his three wonderful, deserving boys.

The clock never ceasing, seven grandchildren soon joined the family. David's happiness in life had reached a glorious pinnacle. If joy is deserved, David was well rewarded.

Unfortunately, wonderful stories do not always promise happy endings.

David often hoped that his children would live long and happy lives. Each time they parted, he worried. Scraped knees and broken hearts were easily mended in their childhoods, but faraway places render a different caution. As adults, David could no longer protect his children from every potential hazard or jeopardy. Safety seemed to be in the uncertain hands of fate.

The tragic call arrived one evening at seven o'clock. There had been a tragic accident on the highway. David's eldest son had been instantly killed.

There would be no undoing the hands of time, no farewell   kisses, no remember I love yous. At the age of thirty eight, his wonderful son had departed the earth. As the black clouds of anguish engulfed him he is certain that he felt his son's presence, hovering above him, as if a sacred spirit of flight.

Grief is all encompassing. It never leaves you, often whispering or uttering the visceral language of loss. It can haunt one's sleep, overwhelm one's thoughts or disturb a fervent prayer. There is no escape from the painful waves and rhythm of suffering. It is a process that must play itself out, for some ending only at their own parting.

A spiritual embrace is the only true remedy for a father's broken heart. One night while sleeping, David found himself between a state of waking and of dreaming. "As I looked into a mirror, a white cat sat on my head and I held a darker small cat in my arms. I noticed a sliver of light emanating from the blind on my bedroom window. As I moved closer to study the source of light, I discovered a shadow and saw an arm with a silver bracelet. I recognized it as the POW military bracelet that my son had always worn.

Suddenly, the large cat transformed as my son and the small cat in my arms emerged into Jeremie's little son. Jeremie tenderly embraced his toddler, kissing and speaking softly to him.

Jeremie quietly turned his face to me, smiling. I knew at that moment that he was happy and well. My father's heart was comforted in knowing that our son remains near to us, especially close to his beautiful twins.

God's grace allowed me this one glimpse into another spiritual realm and for one sacred second a reunion with my son."

Like the father to the son, as the son to the father.

David continues to have dreams of his son. The visits are reassuring and transforming.

Love transcends all parting.

THE LAST PAGES

"Death is no more than passing from one room to another. But there is a difference for me you know, because in that other room I will be able to see."

Helen Keller

Chapter 29

THE ANCIENTS STUDIED the unending cycle of nature
and the seasons. Each new day the sun would rise
in the heavens and transform as   the moon only to
perish each night. Spring brought forth new life and the
splendor of birth. Autumn would welcome the herald of
harvest, rapidly followed by decline. Winter brought a
semblance of hibernation and eventual death.
Miraculously in spring, the cycle began anew.

As went the seasons, the ancients believed that humans
followed the same process, that of birth, decline and
death, only to be awakened and reborn once more in
spring. Endless life was not only paralleled in nature, it
was symbolized as immortality.

In 2009, a study in the United States reported that
49% of the American population had undergone a
sudden awakening, either through a near death ,
spiritual, mystical or religious experience which was life
changing.

Their conclusion was that death is a mere
transformation from one realm of existence to another.

Humans have always pondered their fate after death.
Most world religions believe in an immortal soul that
lives on in some form, eternally. This belief is shared
amongst Christians, the Jewish faith, Hindus, Muslims
and includes tribes of Africa and aboriginal groups in
the Americas.

Archaeological sites confirm that ancient peoples buried their loved ones with grave goods for the afterlife and invitations to the deceased to return to earth in dreams and visions.

Plato and his mentor, Socrates, declared that the soul is not only immortal, but aware, ambitious and driven. They believed that the soul is intelligent and reflects deep thought in the ability to direct and progress from life to death to life again.

In ancient China death was believed to be a mere prolongation of life. They believed that the dead would continue in spirit much as they had done in life. Provisions were made for the departed to use in the afterlife.

After death communications have been well known to the ancients and were regarded as an expectation from the life and death experience.

Today one example can be found in the British Museum and is an actual interpretation of a spiritual visitation inscribed on papyrus. Amazingly, the papyrus dates back to 1350 BC.

Dreams, visions and appearances by departed loved ones have been documented in time immemorial.

Love is the core of human existence. It is the glue that binds, mother to child, generation to generation, the family of man to itself and beyond. Life is eternal. Energy cannot be destroyed and thus presents and represents itself in another form, perhaps in another realm, one more difficult to perceive.

Such evidence transcends ordinary understanding, bridging one reality to another.

So, might it be possible, that after death we are able to return to our loved ones to comfort, reassure and caution? The answer lies in the truth.

A plethora of moving accounts throughout history, some included in this book, reveal a new realization. Humankind is finally evolving to accept things that are often unexplainable, seemingly miraculous and luminous.

Following the death of our son Jeremie in 2012, an illumination began which continues to glow today. It is the light of a divine, loving, existence, one that the presenters in the book and I felt compelled to share with you, the reader.

For those of us fortunate enough to experience communication from loved ones after death, a responsibility to others exists. Sharing these events fosters hope to those suffering from the loss of a loved one, to some who fear death or those who have lost their way, the promise of forever. Immortality validated is the pinnacle of sacred knowledge.

Resplendent communication with loved ones departed and the faith of endless life is the glowing light which will ultimately guide us all home.

Enlightenment is the essence of wisdom. For those lost in grief, the answer is hope, those blind to spirit now may see. Those in search of eternity will now be rewarded.

And we came from the calming darkness into the revealing light. There, we discovered our loved ones, seemingly lost to us, now found.

Let there be light.

ABOUT THE AUTHOR

L INDA KOBLER is the author of the memoir *Sacred Messages.* A registered nurse, she has been acclaimed for her advocacy of the disabled and individuals with severe mental illness. Admittedly, her belief in the power of nursing and the power of words is reflected in her passion for healing and enlightenment.

Her conviction that spiritual, miraculous and mystical events offer transformation, hope and luminescence is well portrayed in the sequel *Stairway from Heaven.*

She lives in Illinois with her husband, David. Always near are her sons and grandchildren. She continues to practice psychiatric nursing in Chicago, Illinois.

For More Information go to:
LindaKoblerBooks.com

Other Books by Kobler

Sacred Messages

"Miracles happen every day.

One must simply open their eyes to see."

CPSIA information can be obtained
at www.ICGtesting.com
Printed in the USA
FFOW01n0503201016
28590FF

9 781615 001309